UNFINISHED BUSINESS

The inspirational story of true grit and determination as Dex Tooke and his crew attempt to conquer the Race Across America

DEX TOOKE

authorHOUSE

AuthorHouse™
1663 Liberty Drive
Bloomington, IN 47403
www.authorhouse.com
Phone: 1-800-839-8640

© *2012 by Dex Tooke. All rights reserved.*

No part of this book may be reproduced, stored in a retrieval system, or transmitted by any means without the written permission of the author.

Published by AuthorHouse   03/16/2012

ISBN: 978-1-4685-5911-8 (sc)
ISBN: 978-1-4685-5910-1 (e)

Library of Congress Control Number: 2012904114

Any people depicted in stock imagery provided by Thinkstock are models, and such images are being used for illustrative purposes only.
Certain stock imagery © Thinkstock.

Because of the dynamic nature of the Internet, any web addresses or links contained in this book may have changed since publication and may no longer be valid. The views expressed in this work are solely those of the author and do not necessarily reflect the views of the publisher, and the publisher hereby disclaims any responsibility for them.

Front photo by Daniel Joder.
Taken between Trinidad and Kim Colorado.

CONTENTS

Introduction xi
Beacons Of Light xv
Chapter 1   The Demons of 2010 1
Chapter 2   Oceanside 13
Chapter 3   The Start: No Pressure at All 23
Chapter 4   Get Me Through the Desert, People! 28
Chapter 5   Yarnell, Mingus and Oak Creek 42
Chapter 6   Where's Bessie? 56
Chapter 7   Wolf Creek, La Veta and Cuchara 68
Chapter 8   My Hallucinatory Friends 86
Chapter 9   Oooh, Missouri 100
Chapter 10   No Sleep for Old Men 113
Chapter 11   The Magic Number 10 136
Chapter 12   Beware the Appalachians 148
Chapter 13   Putting Flintstone to Rest 156
Chapter 14   Trying to Find It 164
Chapter 15   The RAAM Roll Call 172
Epilogue 181
Afterword From Dex 183
Afterword from Joni 187
Appendices 189

Dedicated to the perseverance, sacrifice and passion of my crew:

Joni Tooke-Crew Chief-Domestique
Joe Tooke-Navigator-Historian
Conice Boenicke-Navigator-Medic
Dan Joder-Navigator-Historian
Emily Cooper-Driver
Damaris Ortega-Ford-Driver
Michael West-Driver-Maintenance
Anika Blanco-Domestique
Elaine Lemp-Domestique
Michael Tarbet-Webmaster

The Team Dex Crew, from L to R:
Conice, Emily, Michael T., Elaine, Damaris, Dex, Michael W., Joni, Anika, Dan, and Joe

Thanks for the support to all of the Dexans, The Bank and Trust, KDLK Radio, KGS Bikes and the entire BCFS fund raising committee.

Special thanks to Dan Joder who convinced me to tell my story and helped me to tell it better.

RAAM 2011

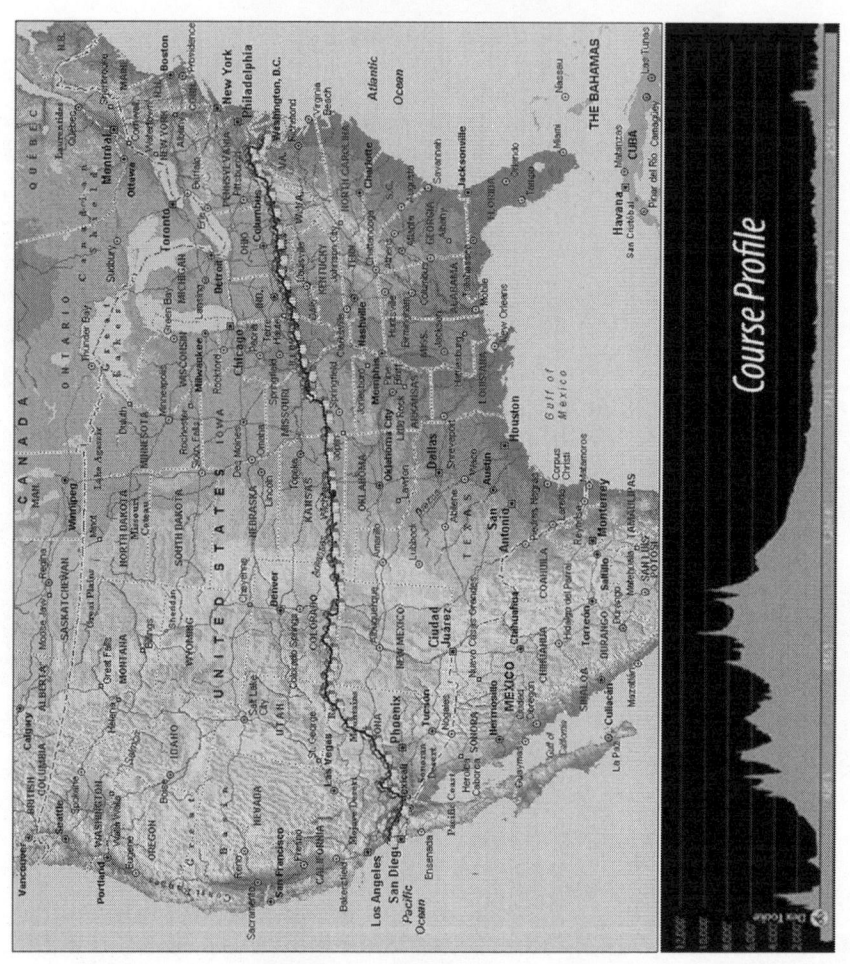

The Course

INTRODUCTION

You are driving across a desert in temperatures so hot that your vehicle's air-conditioner can't quite keep up; your back is drenched in sweat, and the sunshine beating through the windows seems hot enough to literally fry an egg on your dash when suddenly you see movement near the horizon. You wonder what wild animal it could be but when you get closer you are astounded to see a man on a bicycle. Your knee-jerk reaction is that he must be insane and maybe his mere presence triggers a little fear. You think, how could this be, who is this man, how does he survive, why does he do it?

The answers won't be found in highlight reels and they aren't black and white. The only way to truly appreciate the sport of ultra-endurance cycling is by participation.

Ultra-endurance cycling is a sport practiced by people who understand that life is wasted without the pursuit of goals and dreams. To commit one's time, muscles and heart in a quest to ride beyond thresholds that once seemed so distant that they were just previously unimaginable is the core value of ultra-endurance cycling.

While most people have the responsibilities of family, career and quite possibly faith that are simultaneously consuming and rewarding ultra-endurance cycling offers them something more; an opportunity to test themselves in a very personal and profound way in an environment as harsh as they allow it to be.

An ultra-cyclist must turn the pedals one rotation at a time in competitions that can demand over one million rotations, (let alone the training required to prepare). The physicality wears and tears at flesh and muscle which hungrily zaps every iota of fuel in one's body but it is the mind that requires the most maintenance. Muscles seek oxygen and the nutrients in the bloodstream but ambition and desire depend on the soul for fuel.

Riding across a windswept plain on a cold gray day is ugly. Riding in a rainstorm so strong that it tears at one's face is simply brutal, and suddenly becoming afraid to descend a mountain because weariness has stolen one's strength is alarming. To go beyond these boundaries one must find a strength which mere muscles cannot offer. This process clears one's thoughts and taps into the strength of a soul energizing the rider to reach new heights.

Like when an athletic team rises above all their competition because the sum of their efforts far exceed their individual talents, an ultra-cyclist can rise above himself to attain a level of accomplishment so great that it changes the way he views the world and his place in it. Yet this elevated state is not about ego, it is about the humility which produces an understanding of what strength we possess and can summon when necessary.

Men and women, young and old, from all over the world participate in ultra-endurance cycling. They often don't know why, they just know that they must because somewhere, maybe on their sleeves or maybe hidden away in their subconscious they seek a deeper understanding of who they are and what they can accomplish.

If they come up short, they learn and try again because ultra-endurance cycling is not about finish lines; it is not about first place, it is about the journey that starts with a little hope, ambition and a dream. For those who breakthrough and discover something within themselves the journey never ends.

The Race Across America started just like that; by four men with a collective dream that went on to inspire the world. Thirty years after they crossed the finish line, people from all around the world prepare to do the same. And not just on weekends or after work, they prepare with every piece of food they consume, almost every decision they make is based on whether or not it will make them a stronger rider. They sacrifice so many pleasures to prepare because they know there is no escaping the toll that will be extracted and that the sacrifices pale in comparison to the rewards that can manifest. On a journey of a million rotations it is the smallest of details that can grow into a mountain of defeat. The odds are long, the pain unthinkable, yet the reward is not money or fame or ego it is something much more important—it is about discovering the true strength of one's own character and the greatness of life.

Unfinished Business

Perry Stone

The only person on earth to circumnavigate continental Australia three separate times on a bicycle, twice supported by escort crews, once unsupported for a total distance of 42,900 kilometers, with an elapsed combined time of 139.5 days. First two person team entry in 1997 RAAM.

BEACONS OF LIGHT

As the years pass, I turn to my memories to see who I am and where I've been.

Many days have come and gone and I wonder how many more. Most flow as a steady stream, unnoticed under the bridge of time.

I've read that all the days of my life are stored in my mind's reservoir. Some are vague, some only rise if triggered by events or conversations.

Ah, but there are special days, rare days, that stand out as Beacons of Light shining through the murky depths of my memory.

If I take a mental journey pausing at each beacon, I find a common beam of light—each radiates powerful, overwhelming senses and emotions. Overwhelming Joy, Love, Beauty, Passion, Peace, Excitement, Humor, Triumph, and Powerful Fear, Hate, Pain, Defeat, Sorrow.

Some men are content to sit on the bridge of time and wait for chance to surprise them with a special day. Others burn with a fiery desire to experience more than fate brings. Stepping forward to challenge their senses and emotions, they seize the day in hopes of creating a beacon that will remain forever luminous.

Joe Tooke

"There is magic deep in the soul.
Few have the passion to discover it."

Dex Tooke

Chapter 1
THE DEMONS OF 2010

How long has it been since you really, really wanted something? I mean wanted something so badly that you would do just about anything to get it. I'm talking about something that you wanted deep down inside your soul, not something you can just go down to the store and buy. Not something you can Google, then instantly buy on Amazon with a single click. No, I'm talking about *really* wanting something and the only way you can get it is to earn it—even if the price seems incredibly high. Well, in 2010, I *really* wanted the Race Across America.

Make no mistake; the 3000-mile Race Across America, or RAAM, is beyond grueling. It pushes competitors to their physical, psychological and, yes, even spiritual limits. Even knowing this, no one shows up at the start line of RAAM expecting to have a DNF (Did Not Finish) show up next to their name. They haven't invested tens of thousands of hours and training miles just to race part of it and quit. They don't spend $25,000 for equipment, vehicle prep, travel expenses and registration fees just to get a DNF. Yet it happens every year. No matter how well-conditioned or well-prepared the athlete, no matter how strong the will, every year there are RAAM competitors that walk away with broken bodies and broken hearts.

In the 30-year history of RAAM there have been just over 250 individuals who have completed the solo version of RAAM (there are team relay categories as well) within the specified cut-off time. How rare is that? Let me put it this way. There are tens of thousands of triathletes who complete Ironman Triathlons every year. Four times more climbers have walked the summit of Mt. Everest than have completed RAAM. There have even been more than twice as many astronauts in outer space than have completed solo RAAM!

I was a rookie in 2010—a 60-year-old rookie, but a rookie nonetheless. I had never raced RAAM on a relay team, I had never crewed for a RAAM competitor, and I had never been on the course. My crew members, too, were rookies. None of them had ever been part of RAAM in any way. Heck, most of my crew hadn't even heard of RAAM before 2010! And RAAM has never had a reputation for being very kind to rookies. It is very common for riders to compete in RAAM as a member of a relay team before challenging "The Beast" as a solo racer—or they at least have crew members that have either raced or crewed RAAM on previous occasions. In contrast, the entire Team Dex toed the start line at RAAM 2010 with absolutely no RAAM experience for either the racer or the crew.

Then there was the purely physical element. As an ultra distance racer, before that 2010 event, I had never ridden over 600 miles at once. I had no idea how my body was going to react four, five, six, or especially, eight, ten or twelve days down the road. *Could I maintain? How much sleep did I need? How much food did I need? How many miles could I ride in a day once the fatigue, exhaustion and sleep deprivation set in?* All of these were unanswered questions. I mean, after all, you might be able to train for a 300-mile or 500-mile race—but how do you train for a 3000-mile race?

I went into RAAM 2010 on a dime and a dream. I had no race strategy. I figured I would ride when I could and not ride when I couldn't. I thought, *what other strategy do you need in a non-stop race?* I had no scheduled sleep stops or eat stops. There were no crew schedules either; everyone simply took a turn. They each did whatever was necessary at the time it was needed.

In that 2010 event, things started out pretty well—for my standards—and I made good time through the first 300 miles or so. I cramped up in the heat of the Mohave Desert, but who doesn't? Sure, I had saddle sores, but who does RAAM without saddle sores? I just kept pushing through the cramps and riding on the sores, and I surprised myself. I learned that I could ride constantly for longer than two consecutive days. I discovered that my legs, even after hundreds of miles, *did* have enough left in them to carry me up the steep climbs of Congress, Prescott and Flagstaff, Arizona. Things went as well as I could have expected.

I'm not exactly sure why, but in 2010 people all across the country and the world began to follow my race on the RAAM website, and on my personal website, ultradex.net. Michael Tarbet, my webmaster back in Dallas, reported all kinds of responses and activity. During the race, my website had over 7,500 visits and people left over 800 comments. I guessed that people connected with me because they could identify with me—I was the guy next door, just an ordinary guy in an extraordinary race.

That year, it was dark when I passed through Kayenta, Arizona and entered Monument Valley and it was here that I experienced one of my most memorable moments of RAAM 2010. It was during the wee hours of the night as I neared Mexican Hat, Utah, when, in the silence of the dark night, I could hear military-type music approaching fast from behind. I knew it was Jure.

Jure Robic was, and still is, considered by many to be one of the top, if not the top, RAAM champion of all time. He was in the Slovenia military and, for motivation, his crew would play loud military marching music on the follow vehicle speakers while he raced. While Jure is known for being one of the top RAAM champions, he was not necessarily always known for, let's say, his bedside manner. As Jure pulled up beside me, his crew turned his music down so we could talk and visit. With his broken English, Jure expressed to me his goal of breaking eight days in RAAM that year—and no one had ever broken the eight-day barrier. Of course at that time, neither of us knew anything about what was in store for this 2010 group of competitors. Then, when we had finished talking, his crew turned up his marching music and I watched as their taillights disappeared on ahead.

Jure did end up winning RAAM in 2010. But because of the unprecedented weather that lay ahead, not only did he not break the eight-day barrier, he didn't even break the nine-day barrier and it was to be Jure's slowest and last RAAM victory. Tragically, just a couple of months after RAAM 2010, Jure was struck by a truck and killed while he was on a routine daily training ride just three miles from his home in Slovenia. I will always consider it an honor to have raced with the great Jure.

Team Dex rolled into the first mandatory time cut-off station in Durango, Colorado with nine hours in the bank, that is, nine hours ahead of the slowest pace required to reach Annapolis within the time limit. We were so pleased with ourselves that we elected to celebrate by ordering a sit-down meal at the Denny's Restaurant in Durango. Uh oh, big rookie mistake! What we had overlooked was that RAAM is a very long race and anything can and will happen. And, of course, it did.

Not long after our celebratory meal in Durango, and the instant I made the right hand turn out of South Fork, Colorado and turned toward Alamosa, the headwinds hit. *Hard* headwinds. Winds so nasty hard that, by the time I reached Alamosa, I saw RAAM support vehicles and racers, like refugees, pulled over and waiting on the side of the road, because it was simply impossible to stay upright on the bike. I, too, was pulled off the course and waited in Bessie, our big RV support vehicle, on the side of the road as the clock ticked away. I was losing valuable time. When the wind finally died *down* into the 40 mph range, I resumed racing.

Once nightfall came, the high winds turned to storms. That night, as I was climbing to La Veta Pass in the cold rain, race official Jim Harms actually pulled us over to warn us of the terrible, impending conditions at the top of the mountain pass. He told us there was heavy rain and hail at the top and he advised that, if we were to proceed, we were doing so at our own risk.

We decided I would ride until the storms wouldn't let me ride any longer, so I climbed La Veta Pass in the dark and in a cold, wind-driven rain. There were fierce lightning bolts bounding off of the mountain peaks. I could hear hail hitting my helmet, my clothes were sopping wet, and I could not see through my glasses. I was so cold I was starting to get hypothermic.

Finally, in the midst of the freezing rain, my crew took a piece of duct tape and marked the spot on the pavement where they pulled me off the course and then they drove me ahead to the next time station so I could be warmed. Once in the heated confines of Bessie, my wife undressed me and lay nude with me under the thermal blankets trying to warm my body through skin contact. So it was that I went from nine hours ahead of the minimum cut-off time in Durango to nine hours behind. The beast in RAAM had stared me right in the eye and proclaimed, "Game on!"

The fun was over. I still had 2000 miles left to race and the weather continued to pound us. Storms followed us all the way through Colorado and, at one point, Joni actually spotted a tornado behind me as I neared the Kim, Colorado time station.

Just like in the *Wizard of Oz*, the weather didn't get any better in Kansas. The rain continued and there were flash floods with washed out roads and detours for the racers. The RAAM race officials would later describe the terrible weather of RAAM 2010 as the worst in RAAM history.

As my body deteriorated, so did my mental status and I soon became Mr. Grumpy to my crew. Nothing they could do would please me. Sleep deprivation brought on hallucinations; exhaustion brought on paranoia. I started to believe my entire crew was conspiring against me. To catch up with the Beast and get back in the game, I rode for 30 hours straight only to just barely make the next mandatory time cut-off at the Mississippi River—I passed that check point with just an hour to spare.

The long push had not only taken its toll on me, but my crew as well. They were experiencing the same total exhaustion, delirium and sleep deprivation as I; everyone was at their physical and emotional limit. Tempers became shorter as the miles became longer.

From the Mississippi on toward the east coast, I was totally behind the eight ball. I crashed in Ohio when my front wheel was caught in a cement crevice in the road. I went down fast and hard and was very lucky that I didn't fracture any bones. The very difficult climb through the Appalachian Mountains in West Virginia was the hardest thing I had ever done. I was riding like a zombie; I had nothing left.

By then, I was so fatigued that I could not keep up my speed. My off-bike time was increasing and my average mph was decreasing. I was physically defeated. Every muscle in my body screamed. My mind needed rest and sleep. When I arrived at the time station in Cumberland, Maryland I was totally out of it. There, we learned that of the 24 original solo starters, only ten were official finishers—everyone else had DNFed. I was number 11 and the last solo rider still on the course.

As I left Cumberland I knew time was running out; I knew the end was near for me. My mind and my body were totally gone. I made the 11 miles from Cumberland to Flintstone but my speed had dropped to 10 mph and I was so delirious I could not keep my bike moving in a straight line. My coordination was so shot that I had to stop my bike just to take a drink from my water bottle.

Knowing that the four toughest climbs in RAAM were just ahead, I stopped in Flintstone and had a meeting with my crew. I had calculated we were at 299 hours into RAAM. The cut off was 309 hours and we were at 2808 miles which meant I had over 180 miles left to complete. I knew mathematically that I was not going to ride 180 miles over the next 10 hours. I needed at least a two-hour sleep before proceeding and, in the condition I was in, I was sure I would need another two-hour sleep somewhere along the way before I made it to the end. Effectively, that meant I really only had six hours of riding time left to cover 180 miles.

So, I called the crew together and in my sleep deprived, delirious and exhausted state, I told them it was over. I asked them to call the RAAM War Room, as their headquarters in Tucson was called, and tell them Team Dex was withdrawing. The crew understood and, with disappointment, they agreed with me—that is, everyone except my wife, Joni.

Joni was adamant: "I don't care if you have to lie down and sleep. I don't care how long it takes you. And I don't care if the time expires, you are going to ride across this country and cross that finish line, officials or no officials!"

I was so out of it. I could not think. I told Joni, "RAAM is a race. It is not a tour. I respect RAAM and the officials, and I have given this race the best I can do. The race is over."

My crew had fought so hard. They were right there for me throughout the entire race. They supported me in the good times and in the bad times. They were the trailblazers that fought their way through the unknown. They sacrificed their body and spirit and I will forever be grateful.

That day, I made one of the most difficult calls I have ever made when I called the War Room and announced my withdrawal. We were the last solo rider and crew in RAAM 2010 to do so.

With my race over, we then loaded the bike and drove to Annapolis. Pulling up to that finish banner in the car was one of the hardest things I have ever had to do. I had wanted with all my heart to ride my bike to that line. We had fought hard. We went toe to toe with the Beast for a long time. We stared him right in the eye, but we lost: RAAM 1, Dex 0.

The next day I posted a message on my website for the hundreds of loyal Dexans: "I'm a little wounded, but I am not slain. Now I will lay me down to bleed awhile. Then I'll rise and fight again."

Two days later, Joni and I were passing through Tennessee on our drive back to Del Rio, Texas. As we were driving down the highway, Joni was looking back through the notes in the RAAM route book. It was only then that we discovered I had made a crucial mistake while in my exhaustive mental state in Flintstone, Maryland. Team Dex had not been at 299 hours into RAAM—we had been at 289 hours. We still had 20 hours left to race. We both went silent. It would be months before I recovered from discovering that bit of information.

Little did I know then how Joni's reaction to my 2010 RAAM attempt would affect our lives, but it wasn't too long before I discovered her obsession. Immediately after I made the phone call to officially quit RAAM 2010, Team Dex made our way to a motel in Maryland. We were all exhausted and anxious to get a shower and some rest. The crew went to their respective motel rooms and began the process of recuperating. The plan was to get a good night's rest then go to the RAAM finish banner and watch the last of the teams come in.

I went to the room to crash for some much needed sleep. What I got was a much too short, restless sleep filled with delirious mini-nightmares of racing from time station to time station. I would later discover it would be months before I would sleep a nightmare-free night. I would be plagued with restless nights and cold sweats for a long time.

Joni was as exhausted as anyone, but she did not come to bed. She was too upset and disappointed to sleep. I found out the next morning that she had handled her sleepless night in the parking lot of the motel removing race decals and RAAM signage from Shadow, the follow van, and Bessie, the RV. She worked alone in the wee hours of the night. She would remove a decal then cry. Then she would remove another decal and cry again.

At the finish line on Monday morning we arrived just before the last relay team came in. There were officials and a few fans hanging around. Johnny Boswell and his wife, Maurine approached us to visit awhile and they praised me for my effort. Maurine said, "You made it to Maryland. That's a finish in my book." But that didn't make Joni feel any better—it just made her more determined.

I stepped away from Joni for a few minutes to talk with Amy Chu and Sandy Earl. Amy and Sandy were also solo riders who had to withdraw before finishing. While Joni and Joe continued to chat with Johnny and Maurine. Johnny asked Joni and Joe if they would crew for me again if I came back in 2011. Joni barely let Johnny finish the question, before she spouted the words, "Yes, we have to come back and finish this."

Joe turned his head quickly at Joni as if to say, "*You have to be kidding me!*"

Boswell then said, "Let me know if he does come back next year, I want to support his effort. I know he has RAAM in him. The weather got him this year."

I guess that was the minute Joni started planning my next RAAM attempt in 2011. I was mentally not to that point, but she was. It didn't matter if my brother, Joe, was on board or even if *I* was on board. She just knew that she had to begin making plans immediately for the next RAAM. She had been through it once, and so she felt she now had what she needed to know in order to prepare for a successful RAAM the following year.

Joni's RAAM 2011 began the day we left Annapolis and headed home from RAAM 2010. She was already looking at my stats and making notes for changes that would have to happen if I were to succeed the next year. It was more than a commitment to her this time—preparing for RAAM 2011 became Joni's obsession.

She first laid out a priority list from the mistakes we made in 2010. Number one on her list was to go into RAAM with a plan, don't just play it by ear. She knew I was not fast, but she believed that if the crew was more efficient and if I was more efficient, I could finish in the allotted time. She realized that my off-bike time was crucial in RAAM 2010. Eldon had told her he calculated that if the crew could have gotten me back on the bike just five minutes sooner at each time station, I would have accumulated an extra four hours. Joni had confidence in Eldon's math and took it to heart.

She began making lists of things that went wrong in 2010 and tackling each issue in turn. She got on the computer and typed up list after list of things to do. While I still couldn't even think of racing RAAM again, she sat at the computer night after night creating forms and plans. While I was still having nightmares and waking up in the middle of the night with cold sweats, she was on Google Earth studying the route. I was still licking deep wounds, but Joni knew Team Dex was going back—but she didn't push me. Joni patiently waited for me to make up my mind to attempt the race again. I really didn't know what she was doing or planning. People would ask her, "Is he going to do it again?" She would simply respond, "I don't know, but I will be ready if he does decide to do it again."

I was still suffering from my disappointment in 2010, but I continued to ride my bike and she encouraged me. She told me, "Babe, just go do what you do best. Go ride your bike."

I didn't know why I was putting in the miles, I just knew I had to keep riding for fear I would just quit and never ride my bike again. Meanwhile, Joni was reading books on ultra cyclist nutrition. She wanted to make sure I was eating the right food while I was training. I didn't know I was training for RAAM 2011, but somehow she did. I listened to her suggestions about my eating habits and adopted some of her ideas.

Finally, in September, I came to Joni and told her I might want to attempt RAAM again, but not until 2012. She quickly told me, "If you plan to do it again, you will do it in 2011. Too much can happen between now and then. You are in shape now. You just have to maintain your fitness level."

After I raced the Texas Time Trials in September of 2010, I finally came to her and confessed, "Baby, I want to do it."

Once I had committed, Joni became a woman possessed. She had already been working on RAAM 2011 for five months, but now it was official and I was actually saying out loud to her, "I have unfinished business, so I have to go back."

The crew was the next big issue to tackle. While at the Texas Time Trials, Joni talked with a few people from the ultra cycling community to see if anyone would consider helping her crew me on another attempt. She talked with Kayleen Wofford, a respected RAAM crew chief, for suggestions on planning RAAM 2011 and she gathered information and ideas from anyone else who would talk with her. She gained a lot of knowledge, but no crew members. As we talked about assembling a crew, we decided we should reach out to all the Dexans who supported me in RAAM 2010, so we went back to the website blog and looked at everyone who sent comments during the race. After several meetings over the next couple of months, she had a crew of eight volunteers.

Now that Joni had a crew, it was time to train them. She decided to have three crews of three members each—essentially three shifts, to ease the problem of getting sufficient sleep and rest. Each crew member would have a specific duty: driver, navigator or domestique. The pre-RAAM training rides Joni planned were as much for the crew as they were for me as each crew member had the opportunity to practice their assigned position on these long rides. Two of the training rides included extended days, so crew members would get a sense of RAAM-style racing and the sleep deprivation that inevitably goes with it.

The long training rides also gave her a better sense of the strengths of each crew member. After working with them for months, she designated Emily, Michael and Damaris as drivers, Conice, Joe and Dan as navigators, and Elaine, Anika and Joni as domestiques. She scheduled weekly Team Dex meetings to discuss expectations and to review RAAM rules and requirements. She tried to instill in them the importance of their part in the race and, just as importantly, that if they didn't take care of themselves during RAAM, they simply could not take care of me. Our new crew members really had no idea of what they had gotten themselves into, but they were a determined group of volunteers and an amazingly dedicated crew. They all had strengths and special abilities that made the Team Dex crew second to none.

At the scheduled weekly Team Dex meetings, the crew was always very enthusiastic and energetic. The crew and Joni would sit around our dining table with notepads, route books and lists of things to do. Joni would go over detail after detail. She would make task assignments and schedule the next crew for their RAAM-style training ride. She even had each crew member come out to the house and practice driving big Bessie. Each and every one of them had the passion to tackle RAAM. They were anxious to do whatever was necessary and offered their ideas on how to get me across that finish line. While their excitement was genuine and well-intended, when the meetings would adjourn, I would just look at Joni and smile. I would ask her, "They don't have a clue, do they?" She replied, "Of course they don't. How could they? But they are dedicated and they are going to give it everything they have."

Throughout the months prior to RAAM, Joni's preparations amazed me. She worked on RAAM every available minute. During RAAM 2010, I had called many of the shots but, this time, she let me know up front she was the crew chief this year and my shot-calling was coming to an end. She very quickly informed me, for example, that during RAAM, my support vehicle was Shadow, the smaller follow van, not Bessie, the big RV. "Bessie is for the crew," she would say.

Joni worked for hours setting up Shadow as the follow vehicle, drawing up a layout to install a bed in the back for my sleep breaks during RAAM. Emily's husband, Bill, welded a frame for the support and the completed platform measured only 18 inches wide and was barely long enough for me to stretch out. The bed was designed to hover above the plastic storage bins that stored my nutrition, clothing, water, equipment and anything else that I might need on the road. This put the bed at about eight inches from the ceiling of the van. I couldn't believe she expected me to sleep in such a tight space. I guess her reasoning was that I wasn't going to sleep very much anyway and she didn't want me to get too comfortable. Everything in Shadow was for me, and the crew was not allowed to store anything in the van. Each crewmember would bring with them whatever they needed during their assigned shift.

One of the most important things Joni learned through the 2010 experience was to reach out to others. She became fearless, almost aggressive during the planning months for 2011. She tracked down whoever she could to help her answer her questions and accomplish her goals. As Joni continued to work throughout the following months she acted as a lady possessed. She spent every available waking hour preparing for one more attempt at getting her self-proclaimed crazy husband across America in 12 days. She was "ate up" with RAAM. And *that* is what it takes!

Jay Gutierrez: "Dex, may the Spirit that moves all things move you the way you have moved men. Your effort in RAAM 2010 pales all those who leave a trail of blemished victories in our beautiful sport. No, call it not a 'sport' any longer but, rather, reduce it to its most elemental form: a bike ride. Yours this year was truly, truly magical. 'Red lips are not so red as the stained stones kissed by the English dead.' And your victory ride just completed cannot be touched anywhere by anyone, save for by the immortal man upstairs who walks with you. A greater love and honor to cycling, to effort and, yes, to VICTORY, has not, cannot and will not be found compared to what you did this 6th month of 2010 in your 60-70th year! Thank you, ultraDex, for letting us share your RAAM, your effort and your poetic justice to the cycling world of our time. From Vermont, Where Every Ride is a Dance."

Sharon Stevens: "Dex, you were told that 'I've seen RAAM chew up and spit out some very remarkable ultra cyclists.' You said you were one of the not-so-remarkable. May you now realize that with your years of athletic endeavors, and this RAAM adventure, that YOU ARE that very remarkable cyclist, AND a very remarkable person. It is an honor to share this epic journey across America with Dex and the Remarkable Crew. Thank you for a heck of a mesmerizing inspirational honest adventure."

Kevin Saunders: "Dex, I followed you daily and thought it was getting tough in the Rockies, but had no idea it was that bad. You are correct that RAAM is RAAM and this was unprecedented. I know that in any other

RAAM since inception you would have finished with time to spare. If you choose to tackle this beast again, please consider me part of your team! I will give my best efforts to help in any way possible. I have the ultimate respect for you and for your fantastic team. You are all champions who may have been defeated in a battle, but are winning the war. You are an ambassador to cycling and are the example to all that cycling is indeed the Fountain of Youth. I hope you make it to San Antonio soon and can share some stories with me. I am so honored to know you and be your friend."

Shirley Tarbet: "Dex—You have no idea right now of the pedestal you are on in the eyes of so many people. You held nothing back and pushed through pain, blood, sweat and now tears. As others have said—you left it all on the pavement! At the end you stayed true to yourself. Your sportsmanship and high respect for RAAM were in your thoughts in making your decision. You were an unknown—who is now known all across the country, and even other countries. 'Dexan's' are everywhere! You accomplished an amazing feat. You made me feel guilty for going to sleep at night, enjoying the comfort of air conditioning and sitting down to a nice meal. Ha. You paid the price and left over 2,788 miles in the books. Well done. I am so proud of you. Go home, heal up and when you are ready, go for a leisurely ride and enjoy it! You DID ride your dream! Your sister."

Chapter 2

OCEANSIDE

We were headed to the formal "adios-and-good-luck gala" in my home town of Del Rio, Texas, just before our departure to the start of RAAM 2011. The vehicle set up as our follow van, aka Shadow, made a right-hand turn off of Veterans Boulevard onto 10th St. Joni was driving and I was in the right front seat, in what would, during the race, be the navigator's position. Michael was following in big Bessie, while Elaine, Anika, Conice and Em were already at the bank, and Damaris would show up a little later. As we arrived at the send-off party, I rolled my window down to get a better look. Friends and fans had come out this early Friday morning to wish Team Dex good luck and to send us on our way to Oceanside.

"Oh, my gosh! Look at this! Can you believe it?"

My stomach began to feel nervous. There were over 100 people gathered for Team Dex at the Del Rio Bank and Trust. The cheerleaders from Del Rio High School were doing cheers and acrobatics. The Lion's Club had tables covered with breakfast tacos, fruit, cookies, orange juice, water and coffee. Rudy Briones, Del Rio's celebrity DJ, was doing a live KDLK radio remote broadcast.

As Joni pulled the van to a stop, Karen Gleason of the Del Rio *News Herald* began asking me questions before I could even step from the van. The Queen City Belles lined the narrow sidewalk. I held Joni's hand as we walked up the sidewalk among cheers. Everyone seemed to have a camera. I was filled with emotion and overwhelmed. I had never been such a center of attention and I could feel my face blushing. I needed Joni close; she was my crutch to get me through all of this. After all, isn't that what a crew chief is supposed to do?

I wanted to thank and shake hands with every one of the folks there and express my gratitude, and I was scared I would overlook someone. I went straight over to Bill to shake his hand—Bill Cauthorn, president of the Bank and Trust, had been instrumental in the fund raising for my charity, BCFS, in both 2010 and now in 2011. But more than that, Bill, a kind, generous and down-to-earth gentleman, had lent his support to me personally. When we would visit, he always made me feel comfortable. In fact, we both enjoyed talking more about the behind-the-scenes of RAAM and my training than the business end of it. My Mom had raised me to recognize what she called "good people" and Bill Cauthorn was definitely "good people."

Most of my Team Dex crew was there. I saw Anika and Elaine surrounded by several fans, and both women were being inundated with questions. I saw Em kissing her four-year-old son, Wade, and I imagined she was savoring every last moment with him before she had to abandon him for her three-week journey of exhaustion, sleep deprivation and sacrifice. Conice and Michael were chatting with fans, too. Michael, though, looked as if he wanted to leave the party and give Bessie one last inspection. Damaris finally arrived also, wearing her usual huge smile and energetic laugh.

Then something caught the corner of my eye. Over in the shadows, sort of in the background, Merry, Raul and Lisa were standing together, each wearing a smile of pride. They had all served as crew on Team Dex 2010 and a tear came to my eye as allI thought of what they had endured. They had shouldered a sacrifice that no one else would ever understand. They knew the secrets of RAAM and what lay ahead for this new crew. I wanted to hug each of them; I didn't have words for them. And they didn't expect words—there were no words for what we shared the previous year.

The Bank and Trust had a huge billboard electronic sign on its front lawn that kept flashing, "GOOD LUCK TEAM DEX." Passengers in cars would honk and wave as they drove by. After Team Dex posed for photos with the bank supporters and BCFS representatives in front of the billboard, we slowly began to make our way to Shadow and Bessie. It was time for Team Dex to head to Oceanside. A battle lay ahead.

Emily would avoid the long drive by flying into San Diego on Monday while the remainder of Team Dex departed Del Rio for Oceanside on the road. Upon arrival in that westernmost Texas city of El Paso later that day[later that day?], we found Joe and Shirlee, along with their daughters Kristin and Kyndle, grilling delicious steaks on the outdoor patio. This would be Shirlee's second time to lend her husband—and my brother—to

Team Dex. It was a huge sacrifice for her. My mom resided in a living assistance home in El Paso and Shirlee and my sister Shirley would be taking care of Mom while Joe was away during RAAM. our m

Anika and Elaine, being the domestiques and thus responsible for my RAAM food and drink, were quick to show Will, Kristin's husband, how to make a real margarita. Conice was playing with Kristin's one-year-old son Jonah near the pool. Mia, Kristin's four-year-old daughter presented me with a hand painted drawing of me on my bike. It was signed "GO DEX! Mia." We immediately put it on the side of Bessie along with all the other fancy sponsor decals. Joni was in seclusion, continuously working on details to make sure Team Dex was on task to make it to Oceanside on time.

People often ask me where I get my courage and determination. Well, they have to look no further than my mom. I broke away from the Team barbecue for a bit and went to visit her. At 92, she couldn't really grasp the enormity of RAAM or what it actually entailed but that didn't dampen her pride or enthusiasm. She was quick to introduce me to all her assisted-living roomies and her nurses. She was so proud to tell them about her two sons and the incredible journey they were about to embark on for the second time in two years. In the long, lonely miles of RAAM that lay ahead, my thoughts would frequently turn to Mom for drive and motivation.

Team Dex departed El Paso before dawn Saturday morning, June 11th. Joe and I were in Shadow while the remainder of the crew traveled in Bessie. We caravanned throughout the day with the crew frequently rotating and switching vehicles. Finally, having arrived at Oceanside around midnight, the entire Team was totally spent. As we pulled into the parking lot of La Quinta we immediately noticed the heavily decaled support vehicles covered with bike racks of the other RAAM riders.

Sunday morning I headed out on a short ride just to spin and loosen up my legs a bit. I rode the same bike path that I would follow on race day leading away from the Oceanside pier and I immediately rendezvoused with two other solo RAAM riders, Nico Valsesia and Paolo Aste from Italy. They trying to stay looseThis was Nico's 3rd RAAM—I recognized him from a RAAM documentary video and, at age 40, he was a legitimate RAAM contender for the overall win. Paolo, on the other hand, was a RAAM first-timer, or rookie, as they are known in the RAAM world.

While there was a definite language barrier, Nico made it clear to me that his friend Paolo, at 31, was here to leave his mark on RAAM. The three of us enjoyed our ride despite the language limitations.

By the time I got back to the motel, Dan and Em had arrived. Dan had flown in from Boulder, Colorado, and Em, of course, from Del Rio. Team Dex was now complete.

Sunday afternoon was a busy time as the crew attended to last-minute details. Joni, Conice and Joe were washing Bessie while Damaris, Elaine and Anika were inside making sure we had all the right nutrition and hydration to start the race. Michael and Em were up in the room charging cell phones and batteries. Dan was down on the beach shooting photos.

Before cramming my bike into the elevator to take it back to my second floor room, I stopped by the breakfast area and drank some orange juice. I guess I will never know for sure what caused it, and I will forever wonder if orange juice can go rancid, but about 30 minutes after the orange juice, I became very nauseated. Soon after that I found myself hugging the porcelain bowl in my room. It was as if a tornado had hit me. Every bit of my energy was drained as the nausea, vomiting and newly acquired diarrhea took over my body.

My first call for help went to Conice, a physician's assistant by occupation. Conice immediately started me on some oral meds to attempt to control the nausea, but I continued to feel the energy drain from my body. All I wanted to do was get into a bed and be still.

Conice had been the first to volunteer to crew for me in my 2011 RAAM challenge. Handsome, six feet tall with a slender build, he is a man of strong faith. A very dedicated husband and father, his son and daughter occupy most of his attention and focus when he is not working. He runs daily, racing occasional 5Ks and does training runs as long as 18 miles. As Joni and I worked on putting together the Team Dex crew for 2011, we decided we wanted to seek out crew members who had expressed passion during my 2010 RAAM. Em, a long time member of the 5 O'clock Rocker spin class I taught at a local fitness gym, had suggested Conice as a possible crew member. He was one of those individuals who vehemently followed me throughout 2010. Em and her family attend the same church as Conice and his family.

One day I called Conice and requested he meet me at the IHOP Restaurant for coffee and a discussion—it was there we first met. I discussed the possibility of him joining Team Dex as my medic. It wasn't long after that when Joni called a Team Dex crew recruitment meeting at our house and Conice was one of the first to commit and instantly encouraged other possible crew members to do the same.

As crew chief, Joni initially felt Conice might be a good driver for Shadow. However, after one training ride with Conice as a driver, she realized his strengths would be better served as a navigator. His concern for my well-being was evident and his excellent documentation skills were obvious. A navigator had to be someone who could interpret the route book, communicate directions clearly to me over the headset, and keep records at the same time. Conice fit the description and he ultimately proved to be one of the most focused of my crew members.

As it turned out his occupational skills as a physician's assistant were needed long before the race began as I developed some respiratory issues during my training prior to RAAM. In essence, he became my personal physician both before and throughout RAAM.

After the first round of emesis and diarrhea, Conice put me to bed. As medic for Team Dex, he had prepared for everything imaginable and I had actually chastised him at one point because his medical supply bag was so heavy. Now, though, I was happy he had been so thorough.

However, while Conice's medical diagnostic skills were without question, he didn't often get the opportunity to practice those skills. Because of this, prior to RAAM, I had set up a meeting with one of my former paramedic co-workers to work with Conice and familiarize him with intravenous supplies and intervention. Suzie worked closely with him in the weeks leading up to RAAM. Now, as the dehydration of my body due to emesis and diarrhea took its toll, the time came for Conice to put that training to work and he prepared to start an IV of saline to replenish my lost fluids.

While I normally have ropes for veins, they were sunken due to my condition. After several failed attempts to start the IV, Conice finally sought help. from Karl Haller, a solo RAAM competitor from Switzerland, was staying in a room right down the hall from me. Joni had talked with Karl and learned he had with him a field-experienced paramedic as a crew member. Upon request, he came to my room and was able to insert the IV.

After the IV, I remained in bed. The oral meds Conice had given me had the nausea under control, my diarrhea had lessened, and I slept most of the night.

Monday I felt a little better but my movement was extremely slow. I went down to the pier near the start line to rub shoulders with the other solo riders and to be a part of all the pre-race excitement. I also had a media interview appointment that I wanted to keep.

Meanwhile, Joni and crew had taken Shadow, Bessie and all of my equipment down to the designated area for our scheduled 10:00 a.m. RAAM inspection. At registration, each team had been given a *Right to Race* notebook filled with pages of instructions and duties and all had to be completed and signed off by a RAAM official before a team had the "right to race." The most critical part of this notebook was the vehicle and equipment checklist section. Every tail light, head light, brake light, proper signage and race number were inspected. Both my primary and secondary bicycles had to be inspected for reflective tape, lights, batteries and safety. The inspection is a very intense part of RAAM because if something is found wrong, you don't get the "right to race." Joni was very familiar with this inspection from 2010 and she had everything in ship shape with both Shadow and Bessie ready for inspection. Team Dex passed with flying colors and our *Right to Race* notebook was signed.

Monday evening, June 13th, was the RAAM pre-race meeting for all crew members and racers. It was held, as usual, in a gymnasium near the pier, with close to 300 attendees. The 2011 meeting was very special because it marked the 30th anniversary of the race and RAAM legends Lon Haldeman, Pete Penseyres, John Howard and Seanna Hogan were introduced to a standing ovation. Also recognized was Matjaz Paninsek from Slovenia, the late Jure Robic's crew chief. Many would consider five-time RAAM champion Jure Robic one of the greatest RAAM racers ever.

RAAM is a battle. The warriors are referred to as Gladiators. RAAM pushes the Gladiators to their physical, mental and spiritual limits. They go toe-to-toe, hour-by-hour, day-by-day against the Beast. All, even the winners walk away injured, bloodied and scarred. And just like in the Roman days, sometimes the Gladiator wins and sometimes the Beast wins. [It is more man vs. himself than man vs. competitor. man...or something along those lines?] It is at the pre-race meeting that each and every Gladiator is introduced and called to the stage. Each racer is greeted with a standing ovation and cheers, the loudest of which come from their respective crew members.

Before the meeting could end, Joni complained to Elaine that she felt ill as if her blood sugar was low. Afterward, Joni could barely muster the energy to walk up the steps leading out of the pier area. She was driven back to the motel.

Within a short period of time, Joni had come down with the same symptoms that I had experienced. Conice was once again on alert. He now took quick action not only to attend to me and Joni, but also to attempt to quarantine us from the rest of the crew before whatever this was spread throughout the entire Team Dex. To that end, Conice soon had Joni and me isolated in one room.

Joni was pale, diaphoretic and weak, with vomiting and diarrhea. Her veins were even more sunken than mine; they were not easily seen and barely palpable. Since I had more practical experience from my years as a paramedic, I started the IV of normal saline on Joni. There we were, less than 24 hours before the start of the toughest bike race in the world, and the two most critical members of Team Dex, the racer and the crew chief, were both lying in bed with tubes running out of their arms.

There was a Team Dex meeting scheduled for 8:00 p.m. that Monday evening. I was at least not throwing up and I felt it important for me to attend the meeting. Conice thought I probably wasn't contagious and agreed that I would attend, although Conice kept Joni in isolation. Even though things weren't looking good at all for Team Dex, each crew member remained positive and encouraging. This was a meeting that Joni had planned as she was the crew leader, not me, but I followed her meeting notes and did the best I could. Conice and Joni were listening by speaker phone as I talked.

As our meeting progressed, there was a knock on the door. Joe went to the door and then turned and said, "Dex, there is someone who wants to see you."

Bewildered, I walked over to find to my complete surprise, Michael Tarbet. Michael is my nephew from Dallas who I had not personally seen in several years. He had been the Team Dex webmaster in 2010 and I had no idea he was going to show up here in Oceanside. We hugged outside the room, he gave me a fake man-punch to my abs, and then he joined us in the meeting.

It was at this meeting that I poured my heart and soul out to the crew as I tried to explain to them how much this race meant to me and the tremendous emotional and psychological blow of having to withdraw the year before. [and the tremendous??? I spoke from my heart and told them it was imperative I ride my bike under that finish banner in Annapolis this year. I then opened a notebook and pulled out a form that none of the crew members had ever seen before. It was a contract that I had drawn up. I called it the *Team Dex DNF Contract*. It was self-explanatory and would have to be completed in full and signed by each crew member before I would be allowed to DNF RAAM. It read:

Team Dex 2011 Race Across America DNF Contract

Date:
Time:
Location:
Miles raced:
Miles left:
Hours raced:
Hours left:

Has Dex rested within the last 6 hours?

How long was his last rest?

Has Dex been asked what he wants to say in 3 weeks? Has he been reminded about "An Evening with Dex"? Has he been asked about his crew? Has he been reminded of Scott?

Is there a clear and present danger with the safety of Dex if he continues?

Does Dex have a debilitating injury that could harm his future training if he were to continue?

Does Dex have an injury that could cause permanent damage of any type?

Does Dex have a medical complication that warrants stopping this race?

Is there a mechanical issue that warrants stopping this race?

Is there a crew issue that warrants stopping this race?

Explain why Dex is withdrawing from Race Across America:

I agree that Dex should withdraw from the Race Across America (signatures).

Joni:	Anika:	Michael:
Elaine:	Conice:	Damaris
Dan:	Emily:	Joe:

Dex:

    I then told the crew members that this contract was going to be put in a secluded place in Bessie and that I promised to each of them that I was going to do everything in my power to keep any of them from ever seeing that contract again.

Michel Santilhano: "Dex, I hope you get to see this. I will be thinking and praying for you and your dream to be fulfilled. Well done for returning in 2011. The potato is hot, fire in your eyes, love in your heart will power the pedals for Joy in Annapolis!!!!!!!!!!! Hope to shout your name in your ear after Indiana. GO, DEX, GO!!!!!!!!!!!!"

Diana Arrelola: "Your 5 O'clock Rockers ran on Veterans Blvd this morning and of course thought of you and ran for you. May God bless you and you will be in our thoughts and prayers every day. We will spin for you and we will run for you. We love you."

Mayte: "I'm tracking you on GPS and you are making tracks! Looking good, Dex."

Brenda McClintock: "You Got This, Dex!"

Stephanie: "Go, Dex. Shirley called to tell us about you going at it again!! We are so proud of your determination. We're following on the net and sending positive, energizing vibes your way!! Be strong, and GO, DEX!!! Stephanie and Mike Tantimonaco"

Chapter 3

THE START: NO PRESSURE AT ALL

I straddled my bike at the staging area for the start of the 2011 Race Across America. My stomach was queasy from all the nervous tension. I couldn't believe I was about to embark on yet another edition of this 3000-mile race. I wondered, *Am I really here? Why did I sign up for this—again? Why couldn't I just stay home and watch Law and Order rerun marathons? I mean, c'mon! RAAM is the toughest bicycle race in the world. What made me think I was going to become one of the elite few in this world to have crossed from one ocean to another across the entire continental United States? And in under 309 hours? All those people who called me crazy must be right!*

I watched the other racers. It looked as if they were disguising their butterflies as well as I was mine. Michael Tarbet, the Team Dex webmaster, would later describe the atmosphere at the start line as an eerie calm. Nerves were being managed, but the eyes of the riders told another story—similar to the eyes of a bunch of fresh recruit soldiers about to be dropped by helicopter into the jungles of Vietnam. The soldiers were ready to fight, but they all knew the hell that awaited them. All, soldiers and cyclists alike, realized that the same group standing at the start would not all be together at the finish. Riders would smile for the camera, laugh with friends, and chat with other riders, but as soon as they were alone, the task set before them was vividly marked in their eyes and expressions. The warrior spirit was clearly evident among the racers.

While unintentionally imposed and certainly without malice, I felt tremendous pressure. There were hundreds of "Dexans" in Del Rio, Texas and across the country who were counting on me to get to that finish line in Annapolis this year. I had put most of the pressure on myself, of course, running my 2011 RAAM campaign with the "Unfinished Business" slogan. My RV support vehicle and mobile home base camp, Bessie, even had the words printed on her side.

In 2010, I had been the Cinderella of RAAM who didn't quite make it to the Ball before the stroke of midnight. Hundreds, if not thousands of fans from Del Rio, across the nation and literally around the world had jumped on the Team Dex band wagon that year. They were as relentless with their support as I was riding the bike. But I came up 180 miles short of that elusive RAAM finish banner. Now, here I was again. I had publicly vowed to return seeking redemption. Everyone in Oceanside was asking me the same questions: "Are you going to make it this year Dex?" "What are you going to do differently this year to make it across the country?"

To add even more pressure, a couple of weeks before leaving for RAAM, I had gone on the air of the local Del Rio radio station KDLK, on Mr. T's sports program, and announced my intentions of conquering RAAM this year. Listeners called in and texted messages supporting my quest. They couldn't wait to once again follow me online. I was the Nascar driver people watched wondering if he was going to crash in the next turn. I was the cowboy in the arena riding the wild Brahma bull with everyone sitting on the edge of their seat, trying to see if he could last eight seconds without being tossed in the air.

A month before I departed for the start at Oceanside, the local fans in Del Rio had thrown a $100 per plate fund raiser for my RAAM charity, BCFS. It was held at Val Verde Winery and there were even private label Team Dex bottles of wine sold and the event included lavish prices paid for auctioned items. The last item auctioned had been a post-RAAM "Dinner with Dex and Joni" that had gone to an anonymous bidder for $1,000. The event collected over $10,000 toward my charity and there wasn't a person there who expected me to do anything but cross that finish line.

It was 11:30 a.m. race day on the Strand near the pier at Oceanside, California. The sky was as blue as the Pacific. Even though it was mid-June, the air was chilled with temperatures in the low 60s. There was a frenzy of activity near the start area. Wetsuit-clad surfers were walking along the sand with surfboards in arms. Skateboarders were performing their acrobatic leaps near the amphitheater. A man and his wife were slowly pedaling a four-wheel bike with overhead canopy along the sidewalk, their two daughters sitting up front in red helmets, their eyes wide with excitement.

It was just 30 minutes until the start of the 30th annual Race Across America for the females and the 60+ age group. RAAM legends Lon Haldeman, John Howard, Pete Penseyres and Seanna Hogan were honoree starters and would be escorting us for the first 20 miles on the bike path leading out of Oceanside.

Fred and Rick Boethling watched anxiously as the start time grew closer. Fred was the president of the RAAM organization and his son, Rick, the executive director. The Boethlings purchased RAAM in 2006 soon after Fred himself became only the second man in history in the 60+ age group to complete RAAM. At a time when RAAM was close to disintegrating, the Boethlings took a gamble and a plunge, and they salvaged RAAM. Now, the 2011 race was making history as the biggest field ever, with 41 solo competitors in the various categories and over 289 total racers once the relay teams were counted.

The female field included Leah Goldstein from Israel, Caroline van den Bulk from Canada, and the USA riders Janet Christiansen, Debbie Tirrito and Kathy Roche-Wallace. I identified mostly with Janet. This would be her 3rd RAAM attempt and, very much like the previous year's experience for me, Janet had DNFed her rookie year in 2008 in Maryland with less than 200 miles to the finish. She redeemed herself by returning in 2009 to successfully conquer her demons. And as I stood there at the start line, little did I know what fate had in store for Kathy Roche-Wallace and Team Dex in the days to follow.

There had been many years in RAAM when there were no 60+ competitors. In fact, in the 30-year history of RAAM, there have been only four other 60+ solo racers who have managed to complete the race within the 309 hour time limit. But 2011 saw three old geezers at the start. There was three-time RAAM veteran and current record holder for the 60+ category, David Jones, who had returned for his fourth RAAM. Then there was Dave Elsberry, who had won the 50-59 age group in the Race Across the West (RAW) in 2010 in preparation for his 60+ debut in RAAM 2011. Finally there was me, back for my second year in a row. My objective wasn't to beat the other two racers; my only goal was to survive to that finish line within the time limit. I had some unfinished business left over from the 2010 RAAM.

The walkway was jammed with spectators, photographers, media, crew members and race officials. I waved to dozens of fans including three or four from Del Rio who just happened to be in San Diego and came over to see me off. They were holding brightly colored construction paper signs that read, "Go, Del Rio Dex!" My niece and big supporter, Lisa Bliss, had surprised me by flying in from Oklahoma. Ryan Van Duzer, friend, professional videographer and RAAM media veteran, was relentlessly shooting video, attempting to capture the electric atmosphere.

I leaned over the temporary fence for a minute to visit better with Lisa Good, a woman who had been a vital part of my crew in 2010. She was visiting family nearby this year and had come to wish me luck. Lisa had kept a detailed journal of my entire race in 2010 which she turned into a book, *Journey of Suffering*; it gave a first-hand look at RAAM from a crew member's perspective.

My crew was out among the masses. Joe and Dan, the forever historians and photographers, were busy capturing history—Joe, with his professional approach that only years in the photography business could bring, and Dan with his novice enthusiasm and an eye to capture the unexpected. Elaine, Damaris and Emily were busy working the crowd. They looked as comfortable as if they were Prada shopping at Macys. The inseparable Conice and Michael had this "Could we just get this thing started?" look on their faces. The little package of dynamite, Anika, was busy strategizing how she could accidentally bump into one of the young surfer bums. And if there was anyone at that starting area who was any more nervous, scared or sicker than I, it was Joni. With the intense and detailed preparation she had put into this race as crew chief, she had as much weighing on this race as I did.

George Thomas, the RAAM race director, had a wireless microphone in his hand and was introducing the racers one by one. George was wearing a sweat stained cap, khaki shorts and a white Columbia sportswear shirt. The shirt had a breathable mesh screen halfway down the back covered by brushed cotton and an outdated 2010 RAAM logo was stitched over the left front pocket. As if he were auditioning to be the next master of ceremony for the ESPY awards, George would try to think of something clever and humorous to say about each competitor before he would hand them the microphone to say something on their own. I knew exactly what

George was going to say right before he handed me the microphone to speak to the crowd.

"So Dex, are you going to make it to that finish line this year? We are all pulling for you. We know you can make it. What makes this year different from last?"

I took the mike in my hand and gave George and the crowd the same generic answer I had given to everyone else: "I'm not any faster than I was last year, and I'm certainly not any younger. I haven't trained any harder or ridden any more miles this year than last. But what I am is a much smarter rider this year than last. I plan on being much more efficient and having less off-bike time. I expect a huge learning curve from 2010. We were oh so close last year even under the worst of weather conditions. I am planning on giving it everything I have to get to Annapolis!"

It was start time. Silence filled the air and the national anthem was sung. Then each rider was introduced one final time as they began their epic journey. As George called, "Number 383, Dex Tooke", I clipped into both pedals and took off. As I passed George, I heard him say over the microphone one more time, "You have to make it this year Dex!"

No pressure. No pressure at all!

Lily Hernandez: "We pray that the Lord's hands be upon you to shield you from the elements, catch you when you fall, pull you up when you're down, and most importantly, pull you in all the way to the finish line. You are so ready my friend!"

Flora West: "We wish u the best Mr Dex! And crew!!! Yay, it's finally here!!!"

Christine Knight: "And now the fun really begins!"

Chapter 4

GET ME THROUGH THE DESERT, PEOPLE!

The Race Across America is the ultimate bicycle race, a non-stop, 3000-mile transcontinental challenge that begins at the Pacific Ocean in Oceanside, California and ends at the City Dock in Annapolis, Maryland. The key word is *non-stop*; once that gun goes off in Oceanside, the clock never stops. Just because it is 112 degrees in the Mojave, or just because it is hailing in Kansas, or just because you don't feel like climbing all those steep mountain passes in the Rockies, the clock doesn't stop. And, even in my case, just because I was sick and had no strength, the clock still wasn't going to stop for me!

When it came time to clip into my pedals to start the Race Across America, I was already weak, dehydrated and nauseated, and I had been running to the *john* much too often. The five solo females, the three 60+ solo males, and the celebrity pacers stayed together during the first eight-mile "parade zone" along the San Luis bike path, then the racing began once we departed the path. The following 16 miles were totally unsupported by crew so racers had to be self-sufficient until meeting up with their support vehicles at the end of the section.

This part of the route was different from 2010 and the first 16 unsupported miles were much hillier than what I had ridden the year before. I had planned on riding carbon tubular wheels for the most part in RAAM but, since this first section was unsupported, I rode clincher wheels as clinchers afforded me the opportunity for quick tire repair if I flatted. The down side with my set of clinchers was that the rear wheel didn't have a cassette with the appropriate climbing gears. My weakened physical condition, combined with the steep hills and the wrong cassette made my RAAM start a true struggle.

Unfinished Business

Within the first 15 miles of RAAM, I watched in frustration and desperation as the other racers pulled ahead and left me in the distance. You hear of people seeing their whole life flash in front of them when in near death situations, well, I saw my whole RAAM flash in front of me. I saw my hopes, my dreams, my redemption of 2010 vanishing before my eyes. It was like someone took my entire *Unfinished Business* campaign and hit the delete key. The more I thought about it, the more it pissed me off and I started feeling pity for myself. *Of all the times to get sick, why now? What did I do to deserve this?* The disappointment and hopelessness grew with every completed mile. *So much for the Evening with Dex, the Bank send-off party, and the Mr. T interviews.*

Joni had originally scheduled herself as domestique from the start through the first two time stations, but her contraction of my Montezuma's Revenge quickly threw a kink into her best laid plans. The first crew in Shadow would be Elaine as domestique with Emily as the driver and Dan as navigator. They had never worked together as a team. Heck, Dan and Emily had never even met before Dan's arrival at Oceanside for the start. But all three were eager to get this show on the road and do whatever was needed.

Em and crew waited anxiously at the 24-mile point for my arrival, the very first opportunity for racers and crew to rendezvous. A crew member from another team had positioned himself about a quarter mile up the route and would ring a bell to signal a rider's approach. The Team Dex crew kept hearing the bell ring and they would wait with excitement, but it would not be me. Rider after rider came by and still no Dex. They became worried, thinking maybe I had had mechanical problems or possibly was just too weak to ride.

Finally, the bell rang for Dex and the Shadow crew got their initial opportunity to support their rider. The first thing I did was pull over so we could change out my clincher wheels and put on the tubular wheels. The tubulars would give me a smoother ride, contributing less to my fatigue, and the rear wheel thankfully had a much more hill-friendly cassette.

Elaine was thrilled to finally see me. She immediately started stuffing my water bottle with ice and water and she offered me several food options, but I quickly declined them all—my digestive system was still in distress. She sprayed sunscreen on my legs but knew better than to try to spray my face with it because I am extremely sensitive to anything being sprayed or rubbed on my face. Much to my objection, though, she sprayed the

29

sunscreen on her own hands and then with as little intrusion as possible, wiped it on my face.

I was not a happy camper. I was grumpy, irritable and uncooperative. Em would ask me if I needed anything and I wouldn't even respond to her. Kind, gentle hearted, Dan was working furiously to get the wheels changed and I didn't even say "thank you." I was not starting my race on a good note.

Also, to feed my frustration even more, RAAM had a new rule in 2011: direct follow by a crew during daylight hours was not allowed for the first 1000 miles—all the way to Kim, Colorado. "Leapfrog" support was mandatory during daylight hours which meant that Shadow would have to travel at traffic speed while on the road. When available, the crew would find a wide spot in the road and pull over, awaiting my arrival so they could supply any nutrition or hydration needs. With her characteristic foresight, Joni had required all the crews to practice this leapfrog technique on the training rides and we quickly learned that it was much better for Shadow to stay behind me during leapfrog than to be ahead. If they pulled ahead, then it might be a mile or two before they could find a wide spot in the road and, in the meantime, I could have a mechanical problem and be stranded for a period of time before they realized it. By staying behind me as much as possible, they could keep a better eye on me. Occasional jumps ahead were necessary, of course, when it was time for a feed.

The road to Time Station 1 (TS1), Lake Henshaw, California, was a continuous climb up to 2800 feet of elevation with a very narrow shoulder and heavy traffic. The high speed traffic and big trucks did nothing but contribute to my pissed off frame of mind. The key to RAAM is having a good attitude and my attitude sucked at that moment.

As I would ride by, my crew would be pulled over by the side of the road anxiously awaiting to be at my beck and call and to help me in any way. They would cheer me on as I approached, "Good job Dex, keep it up! Everything okay? Do you need anything?" They were totally being there for me—and what did I do? I would just give them a dead, blank stare and I wouldn't say a word. Here were these totally loyal and dedicated friends who had sacrificed their time away from their families and their vacation time to do nothing but support me and I was treating them like crap! I was being nothing short of a whiner, a cry baby.

Team Dex arrived TS1 at Lake Henshaw. 57.2 miles. 5 RAAM hours.

It had been years since I had ridden 57 miles so slowly. By the time I hit the time station, the temperature was nearing 90 and the crew had Shadow parked under the only tree around so I could be in the shade. Dan hurried to my side to hold my bike so I didn't have to worry about where to lean it. Em helped me inside the van, turned on the air conditioner and put a cold towel around my neck. Elaine again tried to get me to eat something. She offered Hammer Gel, Perpetuem, Balance bars—anything to get me to eat, but I was still nauseous. I knew if I ate it would just come right back up. Or worse, it would come out the other end while I was in the middle of all this traffic.

I was still in my foul mood, ignoring anything my crew offered and ignoring all they said. Then I pulled a real boner. A RAAM official came over to me and asked me how things were going. I replied with a huge smile on my face that things were going great. I was cheerful, polite and pleasant with him. Then when he left, the very next second, I was my grumpy self to my crew. They should have abandoned me right there.

After Henshaw, the traffic congestion wasn't quite so bad and, although I still wasn't eating well and was dangerously dehydrated, my attitude improved, climbing to at least a three on a scale of 10. The route continued to climb to 4500 feet at mile 70 where riders encounter one of the most spectacular scenic overlooks of RAAM and the start of a long, steep descent known as "The Glass Elevator."

Here, I'll reveal a deeply personal issue that only those who have crewed for me in ultra races know: I have a serious phobia about descending. This phobia had its roots in an incident on a normal training ride in the Davis Mountains near Alpine, Texas in September of 2005. I was on a steep, curvy descent and traveling maybe 35 mph when a car pulled up beside me. The car did not maliciously buzz me or drive unsafely in any way, but all of a sudden, out of nowhere, the front end of my bike began to shake. I had no idea what was happening or what was causing the front end to go so crazy. The vibration became violent, as if my bike were having a seizure. It became so severe that I felt like I was going to crash for sure and I began to look for a place other than solid boulders to ditch my bike. Luckily, I made it down the mountain pass without crashing but, by the time I got my bike stopped, I was going 10 mph with the front end still shaking like a leaf. In reality, the bike was not shaking at all—it was the adrenaline shooting into my arms. *I* was causing the shaking.

At the time, I brushed off the incident without thinking too much about it. Then, the very next day, on nothing more than a roller of a hill that I ride every day on my commute to work, the same thing happened again. I had been riding a bike for decades and while I wasn't the fastest on descents, I certainly could hold my own and I had never experienced a fear factor before. But ever since that incident in west Texas, I have had to use extreme caution as I go down even the slightest of hills to keep from having another shaking frenzy, which I now call a bike seizure.

I was totally embarrassed about my problem. I mean, here was Dex Tooke, ultra racer extraordinaire, but too chicken to ride his bike down a hill. A grandmother on a mountain bike could pass me going down a hill as I sometimes found myself going 12-15 mph on steep grades and constantly braking to maintain control.

I had tried everything I could think of to correct the problem. I tried distracting myself on descents by thinking of other things, by counting out loud, or by humming to myself. I had even tried tackling the problem head on. Joni once took me to the Davis Mountains and I rode that same descent over and over again. She would wait for me at the bottom of the hill in the van, then immediately take me back to the top to descend again. Nothing seemed to help.

The problem was obviously psychological—it was all in my head. Before RAAM in 2010, I sought help with a hypnotist and I went to several sessions in which she tried to uncover any deep mental problems that could be causing the problem. The sessions helped some, but still in no way was I normal going down a hill.

With a total of over 110,000 vertical feet of climbing, RAAM is all about climbing. However, that means there is also a corresponding 110,000 feet of descending. I have a reputation for being a good climber and many competitors and fellow riders have accused me of being a mountain goat. Too bad I couldn't go *down* a hill as fast as I could go up!

Before RAAM 2011, I again sought help for my descending problem. I went to another hypnotist but still had problems on even generic descents. Then I met with clinical psychologist, Greg Cheyne LPC, MA. Greg was convinced my symptoms of hyper-vigilance, increased heart rate and extreme fear that I would crash, most resembled those of Post Traumatic Stress Syndrome. He suggested I use a technique, Emotional

Freedom Technique (EFT), that is used by many people to alleviate similar symptoms and that worked fast. Greg gave me videos of EFT procedures to review and then he met with me to discuss every detail we could think of surrounding the trauma while using EFT.

While not curing me completely, this training seemed to work best, but I continue to have to descend with the utmost caution in order to prevent the all-out bike seizure. Even on the tamest downhill, I still must feather my brakes; I just can't seem to let my bike roll naturally down a hill.

So, needless to say, I was very nervous as I began my descent of the Glass Elevator—it was white knuckle time for me. The Elevator can be dangerous, a steep, 11-mile descent with 30 mph hairpin curves that take riders from 4500 feet in elevation and 60 degree weather down into the Mojave Desert at 590 feet and 100+ degree heat. The crosswinds in the canyons make the descent even more treacherous. There have been RAAM racers in previous years that have ended their RAAM within the first 80 miles due to a crash on The Glass Elevator.

I could feel the temperature rising as I descended into the desert. As I rounded the curves, feathering my brakes all the while, I looked over the canyon cliffs and down into the valley of the hot Mojave Desert. I could see the little community of Borrego Springs far below and some tiny specks miles in the distance which were actually vehicles traveling on Highway 78 leading out of Borrego. The vista was amazing. After some 20 minutes of what for me was a tense, nerve-racking descent, the grade of the highway began to level out and I began to relax. Phew! One small demon down.

When a racer arrives at a time station, it is the responsibility of the crew to call the War Room, the RAAM race official headquarters in Tucson, Arizona which is manned by RAAM officials 24/7. They record and monitor every racer as well as any potential problems along the RAAM route. When a crew calls in, they must identify themselves, identify their racer by name and number and give the receiving official the racer's arrival time at the TS. The official then gives a return authorization number to the crew member. In addition, crews are required to notify the War Room anytime the racer is off his bike for any length of time over 30 minutes for any reason, whether it be for a sleep break, medical issues, mechanical problems or any other complication. If a crew fails to call in when the racer is down for longer than 30 minutes, the racer can receive a time penalty.

Especially in the rural West, most time stations are not manned, often being nothing more than a parking lot at a deserted strip mall, small store, or post office. It is here that other crews, usually in their RVs, gather to wait for their racer to come through. The time stations give a chance for racer crews to get to know each other, talk about their racer and all the problems they are having and exchange ideas and RAAM stories.

Team Dex arrived TS2, Brawley CA., 146 miles. 11 RAAM hours.

I was still moving at a ridiculously slow pace through TS2. There, Dan and Elaine were more than happy to relinquish their Shadow duties to Conice's crew with Michael and Anika. Elaine told Joni, "I'm glad that is over. This is hard. I had no idea he would be like that!"

For whatever it was worth to them, I later pulled Em, Elaine and Dan off to the side and apologized for my behavior.

From that point on, things started to look up a little bit; the first hundred and fifty miles were under my belt. I remained weak, though, and I wasn't taking in near the needed calories because I was still nauseous and could not keep food down. But, at least it was sliding into nighttime in the Mojave, under a big, fat, full moon, and the temperature had cooled below 100. Night riding seemed to always improve my attitude. With sunset, Shadow was now in direct follow and it was a RAAM rule that during night racing the follow vehicle must keep the racer within the beams of their lights at all times.

The nighttime has always been mine. I do a lot of training during the night and I like the solitude of night riding. There is so much less traffic at night just about anywhere you ride and you can't get much less traffic than at 3:00 in the morning in the middle of the Mojave Desert—and Michael was doing a great job of keeping Shadow's big headlight beams leading and lighting my way.

One of the big improvements Joni had made based on our 2010 experience was in the area of communication. In 2010, I had no way to communicate with my crew in Shadow. We had purchased a cheapo PA system so they could give me route directions but that piece of crap went out early in the race which made communication a total nightmare. Every time I needed anything, whether it was water, food, a restroom break or whatever, I would have to stop pedaling, coast, stand on my pedals, turn around and look at my crew and try to communicate to them, either by yelling or hand signals, exactly what I needed. Even more of a problem was navigating through a town or city. I was constantly having to stand and turn around, wondering if I was suppose to be making a turn or not. It was extremely difficult for the crew because they would have to lean out the navigator's window and yell over the wind noise to try to tell me when and where to turn. In short, it was a major headache.

In 2011, Joni corrected the communication issue with a radio headset. It was the type of headset used by motorcycle riders and it had a small speaker that attached to my helmet which allowed me to hear the crew as well as a microphone that allowed me to talk to them. While the headset had a very short range, at least we could talk when Shadow was in direct follow mode.

So, as we left TS2, Conice was playing his double role now as navigator and medic and he immediately began asking me about how I was feeling and what was going on with my body. After he finished his thorough patient assessment, I asked him to turn on my music. I had two speakers attached to the front of Shadow with an amplifier inside which allowed me to play a MP3 player. With tunes blaring, I got comfortable on my aero-bars and settled into my rut of doing what I do best: cranking out the miles.

We rode through the Glamis Sand Dune Recreational Area under the light of the bulging moon and, while we were going through the area, a RAAM official pulled up beside us. In addition to the officials in the War Room, RAAM also had mobile officials on the race course itself. They were like little DPS troopers hiding behind trees and bushes, constantly watching to make sure a team didn't break any of the rules, always at the ready to hand out those little time penalty tickets. I say all of this with friendly sarcasm because, in all fairness, I was never treated with anything but courtesy and respect from all the RAAM officials. They were there to assure the integrity of the race and to make it as safe as it could be. And our night encounter in the Mojave desert with this official was just that, a friendly check-up to be sure we were being safe and that all was well.

Somewhere after the Glamis Dunes, I saw my first of 11 RAAM sunrises with the orange sun peeking over that eastern horizon. If you are going to race RAAM, you have to love the word EAST! Soon after sunrise, just a little over 200 miles into RAAM, I reluctantly took my first sleep break. I was so weak and exhausted that I was falling asleep on the bike. Taking a sleep break only 16 hours into RAAM was a mental defeat for me. In 2010, I didn't take my first sleep break until Salome, Arizona at 342 miles.

I was falling further and further behind last year's race.

Team Dex arrived TS3, Blythe, CA. 235 miles. 19 RAAM hours.

Joni still wasn't feeling well enough to take a tour of duty so Dan's crew of Damaris and Elaine were in Shadow as we departed Blythe, California. We followed the Colorado River for awhile, then eventually crossed it, moving into Arizona. Dan was waiting on the bridge, taking photo after photo as always and, as I passed, he yelled, "California is DONE, Dex!" Through the remainder of RAAM, this would become a ritual. Either Dan or whoever was on crew at the time would give a yell each time we completed a state.

I was still extremely weak, though, and I still wasn't eating like I should nor was I drinking near enough fluid. I was on the verge of having kidney problems and my calorie intake was way below my standard. With experience, I had learned that my body operates best during ultra racing on about 200 calories/hour which is about the most my body can metabolize without getting nauseous. While on the bike, my nutrition was mostly liquid consisting of Perpetuem, Pink Juice (Iso-Pure) and Ensure, all three of which are similar in nutritional value, providing a good balance of carbohydrates, protein and fats. The domestique of the crew would pre-mix 200-calorie flasks of Ensure and Perpetuem and I would carry a flask in my jersey and try to down a flask each hour. I also occasionally ate a Balance Bar or Cliff Bar. I used water for hydration along with regular intake of Endurolyte capsules and Pedialyte to replace electrolyte loss. V-8 was another good source for electrolytes, but I had to be careful with the V-8 because I could overload my system with too much acid. I never use Gatorade or other flavored sports drinks. To me, they are a very inefficient electrolyte replacement.

Elaine was trying her best to get me to down my regular dose of Perpetuem, but I just wasn't buying it. By the time we arrived in Parker, Arizona, the desert heat was getting really nasty and I was really out of it. My crew was doing everything they could to try to get me to eat and keep me on the road.

Team Dex arrived TS4. Parker AZ. 287 miles. 24 RAAM hours.

Besides being sick, I was also mentally defeated. The least mileage I had ever ridden in a 24-hour bike race was 320 miles—and that was my rookie attempt at 24 hours. Now here I was in the biggest race of my life and I had only completed 287 miles during the first day. The first 24 hours in RAAM, while one is still relatively fresh, is every racer's opportunity to put money in the bank and as far as I was concerned, I had just written a hot check!

Bessie rendezvoused with Shadow at the Circle K, the Parker TS and after Conice and Joni talked it over they decided I should try to take a sleep break. Conice thought it would also be a good opportunity to stick an IV in me for hydration purposes.

So as to not disturb me as I rested in Bessie, and at the same time to get out of the heat, everyone except Conice crashed the Circle K. There was a beer display that was just the right height for them to sit on and have a mini Team Dex meeting and social gathering. The crew was exhausted and giddy. For the first time in a while, they had some bars on their phones so they caught up on their phone calls, text messaging and Facebook postings.

Then the play began. Elaine had a photo of Joe on her phone which showed him holding my bike. He had on cool shades, his cap was turned around backward and he was wearing a flattering muscle shirt. Elaine showed it to Damaris and Anika and made the comment that she was keeping this one. She then tagged the photo as "Stud Muffin" and posted it on Facebook. Elaine continued on her usual roll, spitting out sarcastic humorous remarks like she was Leno on *The Late Show*, finally summing it all up with a kindly reference to me: "I figured this wasn't going to be easy, but I didn't know he was going to be Mr. Grumpy!"

Joni replied, "You ain't seen nothin yet. Just wait until day four or five!"

The intensity of it all affected everyone differently. Michael, a Mountain Dew junkie, was now buying the caffeine-laden drinks by the six-pack. Anika snuck off to the ladies room and, although she wouldn't announce it until later, she had made a personal RAAM goal of her own: she was going to take a dump at every single RAAM time station—and she was off to take number three of 55. On the opposite side of the coin, Em was so nervous and her system was so out of whack that it would be days before she took her first one.

Inside Bessie, I collapsed on the bed and Joni arrived to help me remove my double shorts while Conice busied himself setting up the 1000 ml bag of lactated ringers for the IV. I tried to go to sleep, but it just wasn't happening. I lay motionless on the bed with my eyes closed, resting as much as I could as the IV fluid flowed into my veins. I don't think I ever did go to sleep. If I did, it was a very short and very shallow sleep.

Once the IV was completely infused, Joni began to help me get my shorts back on. I was already developing saddle sores and she medicated them with her special potion, but as soon as I stood up, I had the urgent urge to crap. I rushed to the little cubby hole of a bathroom in Bessie and had a man-sized diarrhea episode. I then went back to Joni so she could re-medicate my butt and get my shorts back on. But again, before she could finish, I had another episode. This depressing act repeated itself a total of four times. Whatever fluid and hydration benefit Conice had given me through the veins had just been flushed into Bessie's waste reservoir.

By the time I mounted my bike to depart Parker, I had lost nearly two hours of non-sleep time, and that is a killer in RAAM. Other than quick stops for eating, sleeping is the only reason you should ever be off your bike in RAAM—and I had just sacrificed two entire hours.

There isn't a RAAM veteran around who won't tell you that one of the most intimidating parts of RAAM is getting through the desert; it strikes fear in everyone. The desert heat can zap a racer, dehydrating him or her to the point that it can take days before the body can catch up. Before RAAM 2010, I had sought advice from RAAM veteran Kevin Kaiser who was eager to help me and soon became not only one of my mentors for RAAM but also my inspiration. Kevin had told me how, in 2009, the desert had beaten him up so badly that by the time he reached Sedona, Arizona he was nearly two hours below the minimum pace needed to finish. He was devastated at that point and actually had already mentally quit the race. But, he kept going and was finally able to recover once he hit Colorado and Kansas and he eventually finished well within the time limit in fifth place overall.

About a month before RAAM, I sent out an e-mail to my crew expressing my concern about getting through the desert. I explained to them physiologically what occurs to the body in extreme heat and gave them specific instructions on what to do and how to take care of me. I also made them a promise: "Get me through the desert, people, and I will ride for you."

Now we were in the heat of the battle, literally. It was mid-afternoon local time and Team Dex was pushing on through the brutal desert furnace. For the next 56 miles to Salome, I would be on a heavily traveled Texas-like chip seal road that climbed from 400 feet of elevation up to over 1900 feet. Joe's crew of Em and Joni had to monitor me very closely. At one point, the thermometer in Shadow read 115 degrees and I could feel the heat scorching my legs as it radiated off the pavement. There was no telling what the temperature was rising up off of the asphalt.

The traffic was heavy and Shadow was in leapfrog and could not protect me. Eighteen-wheelers would zoom by, inches away, with their draft blowing me sideways. To top it off, we hadn't gone but four or five miles when the smoke from the huge Tucson wildfires moved in on us. I stopped and Joni put a surgical mask over my mouth for protection.

The heat was scary. With my paramedic background, I was very familiar with all the signs and symptoms of heat stroke and there wasn't a one of them that I wasn't experiencing. I would ride for maybe five minutes then I would stop. Joe would sit me in his navigation seat in Shadow with the air conditioner going full blast while Joni put ice towels around my neck to try to cool my core temperature. Joe then stood out in the hot desert air holding my bike while I cooled down inside the van. Then, as I readied to go again, Joe, my loving and caring brother of infinite wisdom and RAAM experience, put his arm around my shoulder and asked, "Are you feeling good?"

I blurted out, "You got to be friggin kidding me!"

I was extremely close to heat stroke and I actually feared for my life. Since I hadn't been able to sleep at Parker, I was also getting extremely sleepy. I had ridden just 30 miles since I left Parker when Joni called Bessie and asked the crew to come rendezvous. She decided to get me out of the heat and put me down to sleep, so she called the War Room to let the officials know I would be down. I slept for an hour in Bessie.

After my short nap, I got back on my bike, but I couldn't tell if the sleep really did me much good. In keeping with the state of affairs at the time, and inspired by the name of a little place called Hope, Arizona that we had just passed, Joe took the opportunity to yell out at me, "You are beyond Hope now!"

And he expected me to laugh?

As the sun set and the temperature dropped below 105, I began a steep climb about six miles outside of Salome. Em would later say she thought this was the turning point in the race for me. As the sun went down, Shadow went into direct follow and she cranked up one of my favorite 5 O'Clock Rockers songs, *Get Out of My Car*, by Billy Ocean. I stood and danced on my pedals as I made my way up the climb. Now this was Dex . . . climbing into the night. Maybe I can do this!

Team Dex arrived TS5. Salome, AZ. 342 miles.
32 RAAM hours.

It had taken me eight hours to ride from TS4 to TS5, just 56 miles away. Welcome to the desert, people!

Christy-Trevor Hill: "Dex, Trev and I are so incredibly proud of you!! You are a true inspiration!! We will follow you every mile of the way! Sending you all our love!"

Melissa Lopez: "He . . . he . . . tell Dex our customers keep asking if he's on vacation, laying out on a beach somewhere!!! I just laugh and tell them about RAAM and say it's Dex's version of a dream vacation. GO, DEX, GO!!"

Dalia Blanco: "Get my little girl out of Arizona :) Right behind you in San Antonio!!!"

Roger and Kelly Bollinger: "Keep on going, Dex. You can make it this year!!! Your heart and soul are in it. Keep the updates coming!! Praying for you and the crew . . . all of you hang in there. Be safe and keep all the spirits high. YOU CAN DO THIS, DEX!"

Tony Hernandez: "Time to find the soul on that bike and ride it like the wind my friend!!! God Speed!!!"

Venita Tooke Butler: "If Dex can handle the Arizona heat and the Colorado mountains, then he can handle ANYTHING! Go, Dex!"

Chapter 5

YARNELL, MINGUS AND OAK CREEK

Many might assume, since I am a crazed ultra endurance lunatic, that I must have been an athlete my entire life, probably excelling in track or cross country in my high school years, but the truth is quite the contrary. Not only did I never run track, I was hardly into sports at all. I was never very good at Little League baseball and was always the last guy picked for team sports. As the runt of my senior class—five feet tall and 98 pounds—the almighty sport of west Texas football was out of the question. I did play some tennis during high school but would hardly say I excelled.

At age 28, I was smoking over a pack a day and I was usually in a bar every night after work. I was still young enough to know better but I thought I was invincible. So, just to reassure myself that I was still in shape, one night I went out to the local quarter-mile track to run a mile. Boy, was I surprised! I couldn't even run one time around the track without being out of breath and having to walk. I found out real quick that I was overdue for a lifestyle change.

So, instead of going to the bar after work every night, I started going to the track. I would walk the straights and run the curves, walk the straights and run the curves. I continued to do this until I could finally run a complete lap without stopping. I was so proud of my progress that I continued to go to the track every night until I could run a complete mile. Keep in mind that I was still smoking while doing this. I had no intention of quitting smoking; that wasn't my goal.

Bill Dayton, a close friend who had self-designated himself as my coach would tell me how often and how far I should run. Bill told me that I should build up my distance until I could run for 30 minutes straight. I told Bill, "Thirty minutes? Are you crazy? That's the length of a whole TV show! Nobody can run that long!"

It wasn't until after I started doing 30-minute runs that I finally put the cigs down. I didn't want to stop smoking, but I wanted to run more than I wanted to smoke, and smoking was hindering my running. That first 30-minute run turned into a new lifestyle of aerobic fitness. I started racing 5K and 10K events, and even marathons. Then, I bought a bike and started racing triathlons and from triathlons I moved up to running ultra distance races. I once ran 101 miles in 24 hours at a race in Plano, Texas. Now, 30 years after that first night of running the straights and walking the curves, here I was in a 3000-mile non-stop bicycle race. Life can certainly be curious.

Conice's crew of Michael and Anika was on duty in direct follow as we left Salome, Arizona and I was in better spirits riding in the cooler night air. *Hello darkness my old friend, I'm here to talk with you again.*

Conice did his best talking to me through the headset, trying to keep things as light as possible in an attempt to keep me awake and pedaling.

About three or four miles out of Salome I noticed a California King Snake crossing the road. I recognized the snake easily from previous experience. When Joni and I lived near Dallas back in the 1970's, I worked closely with reptiles in association with the Dallas Herpetological Society. I cared for and worked with all manner of snakes, including most of the highly venomous varieties. I pointed the snake out to Conice as I rode past it and told him it was a *Lampropeltis getula californiae*. Conice, not knowing my Herp background, just said, "Yeah right!"

It wasn't long after that encounter when a RAAM media car pulled up beside me in the middle of the night and talked briefly with me as I rode. I didn't look toward the camera because the bright camera lights blinded me. They then zoomed ahead and I thought they were gone, but they had just gone up the road a piece to set up for a video shot as I passed by.

The 52 miles from Salome to Congress was pretty much all climbing, with the first 25 miles out of Salome, on US Highway 60, on a pretty good surface. But then we made a left onto SR 71 and the road surface went to pot. It was so rough it made me homesick for the Texas chip seal. Michael did an awesome job of keeping me in the headlight beams so I could avoid the largest of the land mine pot holes.

Team Dex arrived TS6. Congress, AZ. 395 miles. 37 RAAM hours.

Not only was Congress one of the few continuously manned RAAM time stations in the West, it was also one of the best and neatest. Of course, it is in the core of the desert and temperatures soar during the day, so they have access to a huge outdoor above ground pool so riders and crew can cool down if desired. This time station also had a T-shirt trading tradition. RAAM racers would bring T-shirts from their clubs and races they have done, drop them at the time station and exchange them for T-shirts that other riders from all over the world have dropped off.

Bessie and crew brought T-shirts from DR FART and my 5 O'clock Rockers to share. DR FART, aka Del Rio Fitness and Racing Team, is a small group of local riders in Del Rio with a huge group of satellite members all over the world. Laughlin Air Force Base (LAFB) is located in Del Rio and, through the years, cyclists and runners who have been stationed in Del Rio have joined DR FART then, after their tour of duty there, they are scattered across the nation and the world.

The early morning spin class I teach at the local fitness gym, referred to as the 5 O'clock Rockers, is a very dedicated and disciplined group. How dedicated? Well, even though these classes start at five a.m., many Rockers show up early just to get their choice of bike. I crank up ZZ, Guns-N-Roses, Van Halen and Led Zeppelin—it is a hoot and a great cardio workout. Lily Hernandez substituted for me during my RAAM training absences. She and the Rockers were a huge support.

I spent less than ten minutes at TS6. Elaine had eggs waiting for me and I inhaled them along with some watermelon. I was finally eating! To emphasize the importance of this, when Team Dex had arrived in Oceanside, I weighed 155 pounds, but when Conice weighed me in Parker I was at 141 pounds. I had lost 14 pounds in the first 24 hours of RAAM! Now it was time to gain some of that weight back. From here on I became a human garbage disposal and pity on anyone who left any food lying around that they didn't want scarfed up!

Dan's crew of Elaine and Damaris took over in Shadow as we departed Congress at about 4:00 a.m. Eastern Daylight Time. Why do I mention Eastern time in Arizona? For simplicity, and to avoid confusion when reporting information to RAAM headquarters, all times in RAAM were kept in EDT regardless of the time zone you were in. That made it 2:00

a.m. local time as Team Dex left the desert basin behind. Good bye and good riddance as far as I was concerned.

As for the RV, due to the severe climbs with narrow, curvy roads on the race route, Bessie and crew were required by RAAM officials to take an alternate route from Congress to the next time station in Prescott, Arizona.

There were over 110,000 vertical feet of climbing in RAAM and this is where the climbing would really begin—we wouldn't see flatlands again until eastern Colorado and Kansas. For the next 800 miles, I would be racing through the mountains of northern Arizona and the Rocky Mountains of Colorado.

Most immediately, I faced two major climbs before arriving at the Prescott, Arizona time station. The first, the Yarnell grade, climbs 1800 feet in 7 miles. After leveling out just a bit, the second, longer climb, over the last 25 miles into Prescott, would average more than 130 feet of climbing per mile. This was the most difficult climbing west of Maryland.

Also, Team Dex was now in Dan territory. Dan lived in Arizona for years and had ridden every one of these roads and climbed every one of these mountains, so I couldn't have asked for a better navigator or historian. From Boulder, Colorado, and close to six feet tall he was frequently described as "skinny" by most, but in a positive way—and no one could help but notice his flaming red hair. I first met Dan back in the early 90s when he was stationed at LAFB as a T-37 instructor pilot. Dan and I would train and race together, but Dan's racing ability was way over my head and I could never keep up with him. He was a legitimate Cat 3 road racer and now, at age 53, was considered one of the top age group racers in Texas. He retired as a Lieutenant Colonel from the Air Force and has lived an extremely interesting and exciting life all over the world.

Dan had his own style of navigating. He was meticulous with his route directing and would give me a heads up on upcoming turns, railroad crossings and route changes as much in advance as possible. This was nice, but what made him unique was his story telling. Dan would get on the PA system and weave a story that would help me get my mind off the endless miles and my ever present saddle sores. His voice was soft and easy to listen to, not unlike the late night syndicated radio host Delilah, the queen of sappy love songs. His stories were always interesting and captivating, not only to me but also to Elaine and Damaris. They would both sit mesmerized as Dan would tell his tales.

One of his favorite storytelling subjects was about his childhood friend, Rik Fritz. Apparently Rik was endowed with nine lives and, in his exciting, adventurous life, had already used eight of them. In the wee hours of the night, when I would really need to stay awake and stay on the bike, Dan would tell about how Rik, as a kid in junior high school, had been bitten by a rattlesnake and almost died because of an allergic reaction to the antivenin. Then there was the story of how Rik had fallen 80 feet down a cliff in these same Arizona mountains yet still found himself alive, dangling at the end of the climbing rope that saved him.

Stories aside, the eggs and watermelon back at the time station must have been exactly what I needed because the climb up the Yarnell grade was easier than it should have been. When I got to the top, I asked Dan, "Was that it? Is it over?"

From there we started a gradual 12-mile descent before we began the 25 miles of difficult grades and snaky turns from Wilhoit to Prescott.

There is an advantage to climbing at night. At night you can only see what lies ahead in the beams of the headlights, so you don't see how steep the grades or how long the climbs. All you see is that little white path in front.

Unfortunately, I typically get my sleepiest right before dawn and the last time I had slept had been in the desert outside of Parker. I was getting extremely sleepy but I did not want to go down, so Dan was doing anything he could to keep me awake. I was so sleepy I was weaving on the narrow roadway, so Dan fell back once again on his Rik Fritz stories. This time, he related the time Rik was preparing to fly down to a ritzy golf course in his hang glider but, before he could get completely strapped into his glider, his foot got caught in one of the side wires and the glider pulled him off of the cliff. Rik suffered a severe laceration to his leg and a broken arm, and was air-lifted off the mountain by a medical helicopter.

Dan then read Facebook and ultradex website comments to me in an attempt to not only keep me awake, but also to motivate me. The comments would take my mind off my misery. Some comments made me laugh while others stirred deep emotions of pride.

I kept struggling up the hills ever so slowly. I began hallucinating and imagining things and people that really weren't there. At one point I imagined I saw a small Dr. Pepper bottle with little legs and feet running across the road in front of me.

Then Dan did something that scared the living crap out of me. I was climbing up one of the steep grades not traveling over 6 or 7 mph, lost in my own hallucinatory world, when all of a sudden, out of nowhere, Dan appeared, running right beside me, screaming in my ear. I thought I was still hallucinating and had gone out of my mind. He had jumped out of Shadow and was chasing me on foot as I climbed. He was sockless and wearing sandals as he ran beside me. I don't know how far he ran but it certainly woke me up. After a long, difficult night, I was able to make it through the dark hour before dawn and finally see the sun beams hitting the mountain tops in front of me.

I will always consider not going down for a sleep that last seven or eight miles as I climbed into Prescott as one of my small victories over "the Beast" in RAAM.

Team Dex arrived TS7. Prescott, AZ. 441 miles. 42 RAAM hours.

Bessie and crew were waiting for us at the Prescott time station in the Walmart parking lot when Shadow and I arrived under a bright, early morning sun. Em had breakfast waiting for me upon arrival. I ate eggs and more eggs. I put cheese on my eggs. I put honey on my eggs. I ate burritos. I drank milk. I drank Vitamin water. I ate and drank everything I saw and could get my hands on. I had pushed through my sleeplessness and decided I would continue out of Prescott without taking a sleep break.

Joe's crew of Em and Joni took over Shadow duties while once again the rest of Team Dex and Bessie would have to travel an alternate route due to severe grades and narrow roads on the race route. Of course, with daylight, that meant Shadow was back in leapfrog mode, so I was once again on my own—my security blanket was gone. I am a very high maintenance rider and once I reach exhaustion and the sleep deprivation sets in, I get very lonely on the road. I want people close by. I want someone to talk to. I want company so I can share my misery. I want someone to be there to hear my complaints. In leapfrog I don't get to share.

It was by this point that my crew deemed me the "Gosh dang it!" king of RAAM. While I have no idea how many times I repeated that phrase during RAAM, you can ask any crew member and they can probably tell you. "Gosh dang it!" was my way of coping with everything from frustration, to exhaustion, to traffic, to hills, the wind, to debris in the road, to dozing off to sleep on the bike and anything else that irritated me. This was my way of handling it all. I know it wasn't a very positive technique, but it seemed to work for me.

I would be climbing and I would have just topped the crest of the hill. I would look ahead and there would be another climb even steeper than the last one: "Gosh dang it!"

I would be in heavy traffic and a car would buzz me: "Gosh dang it!"

I would be riding on a debris-littered shoulder and my front tire would run over a huge rock: "Gosh dang it".

A wind gust would blow me sideways on the road: "Gosh dang it!"

I would be so exhausted that I couldn't get my leg warmers on: "Gosh dang it!"

RAAM isn't always about fun or enjoyment or beautiful scenery. Sometimes it's about Gosh Dang It, Gosh Dang It, Gosh Dang It, Gosh Dang It, Gosh Dang It, Gosh Dang It, Gosh Dang It! It was just my way of getting through the whole thing.

From Prescott to the next time station in Cottonwood, Arizona there was one big obstacle in the way: Mingus Mountain. I entered Prescott National Forest and began a 12-mile climb up Mingus on a narrow, winding road that eventually led to an elevation of 7000 feet, the high point of the climb being the top of Haywood Canyon at Potato Patch. I then descended through the quaint, historic, ex-mining, artist town of Jerome, Arizona—a town that, in 2010, was voted by my crew as the number one spot in RAAM that they would like to go back to visit.

The snaky descent down to and through Jerome brought out my downhill demons once again. The grade was steep with hairpin curves and the road surface was extremely rough with huge potholes to avoid. Shadow was in leapfrog so I was on my own. I got very nervous as I started the descent and was being excessively cautious. Any other rider couldn't wait to reap the rewards of their hard work of climbing with this fast and effortless descent—to most racers this is the fun part of riding. At the very least it is a time of recovery. But, for me the descent was very stressful and filled with tension. My shoulders were tight, my knuckles were white and my eyes were wide with fear. In many ways, the down hills took more out of me than the climbing. Heading down to Jerome, I was constantly feathering my brakes. At a time that I should have be recovering, I was working. At a time when I should have been effortlessly riding at 35+ mph, I was barely going 15 mph.

Some local riders passed me going down the hill as if I were standing still. It would scare me even more every time I would meet a car on the narrow road. But the most scared I would get was when a car would pass me. It was all I could do to keep from having one of my bike seizures.

Joe and Joni were very familiar with my fear but this was the first time Em personally witnessed it and it embarrassed me for her to see me like this. Em had held me up on a pedestal since RAAM 2010—I had become her hero. Now, she was seeing her hero as a coward.

The road from Jerome down to Cottonwood offered amazing vistas and overlooks. Shadow pulled over at many of the pull-outs so Joe could take photos. After one of the pull-outs, and true to the RAAM rule that small things will constantly go wrong and big things will often go wrong, Joe noticed his phone was missing. So, Shadow turned around and traced back uphill toward Jerome, stopping at each pull-out. Luckily, they found it.

Team Dex arrived TS8. Cottonwood, AZ. 483 miles. 46.5 RAAM hours.

It was about 11:30 a.m. local time in Cottonwood when I arrived at the time station and there were three things I needed: I needed to eat, I needed to sleep and I needed different wheels on my bike. Joe bought some sub sandwiches at the grocery store, I ate, then immediately crawled up into the narrow, foam-padded area in the van that Joni called a bed and went down for a 30-minute sleep. Em, Joe and Joni waited outside the van while I slept so as not to disturb me.

The third item on my need list—a wheel change—was more complicated. From Cottonwood, we would be changing road direction as we headed to Sedona and eventually to Flagstaff. The winds were picking up and gusting with a strong cross wind. Up until then, I had been riding some deep dish Reynolds carbon tubular wheels—nice, light equipment, but not ideal for windy conditions. Joni called Kevin Saunders of KGS Bikes in San Antonio for advice and, sure enough, he suggested I get off the Reynolds wheels during the crosswind section and switch to the tubular Topolino wheels. The only problem was that the Topolino wheels had the wrong gear cassette for the upcoming climbs and the tool to change the cassette was in Bessie on an alternate route.

It was time to improvise. Em pulled out her smart phone and located a bike shop in Cottonwood, of course, nowhere near the RAAM route. As crew chief, though, Joni made the decision that she would put my clincher wheels on my bike and I would ride alone toward Sedona while Shadow and crew went to the bike shop to get the tool to switch out the cassettes on the Reynolds and Topolinos. So, I departed Cottonwood without support and made my way alone along State Route 89A and the beginning of a 40-mile climb.

The traffic was heavy and the winds were gusty. I kept looking in my helmet rear view mirror at all approaching cars, watching and hoping Shadow and crew would show up soon. I watched and watched. It was like watching a clock. Every time I would see a silver car approaching, I hoped it would be them. I had made it all the way to Red Rock State Park when I finally saw Shadow in my rear view mirror but, since we were in leapfrog mode, they zoomed by at 70 mph in search of the first available pull-off area. Joni had changed the cassettes and, once I stopped at the pull-out, she put the much lighter Topolino wheels on my bike for the remainder of the climb to Sedona and Flagstaff.

The traffic in the red-rock tourist town of Sedona was very heavy with cars everywhere. *What were all the cars doing on the road? Why can't it just be bicycles? Gosh dang it!* I finally got out of Sedona without incident and continued the Oak Creek Canyon climb toward Flagstaff, passing Sterling Spring, headwaters of Oak Creek. The steep and beautiful Oak Creek mountain switchbacks through the red rock from Sedona to Flagstaff are part of the legendary climbs of RAAM.

As I approached the outskirts of Flagstaff, I thought to myself . . . *I just climbed three of the toughest climbs in Arizona: The Yarnell Grade, Mingus Mountain, and Oak Creek Canyon to Flagstaff. These are climbs that many cyclists probably have on their annual bucket list—and I just did all three in less than 24 hours. Welcome to RAAM!*

Flagstaff was the first good-sized city on the RAAM route. Traffic and navigation was extremely difficult even under the best of circumstances, but under the duress of exhaustion and sleep deprivation, it was even more difficult. In-town navigation was doubly tough with many turns coming in quick succession.

From the very first time I had heard of the new leapfrog requirement for the first 1000 miles of RAAM, my main worry had been navigation. How was I going to navigate through the congested areas? Sure, my crew could drop members off at key intersections, or the van could wait for me and yell at me as I passed by. But, from my experience in 2010, I knew both of these methods could be hit and miss at best.

So, to correct the navigation problem, I devised a flag system. Joni bought various colored plastic table cloths from Dollar Tree which she then cut into 12" x 16" rectangles. She then attached the flags to 3/4" diameter wooden dowels. I took a black marker and, on the blue flag, I wrote, "Right turn Clyde!" On the yellow flag I wrote, "Left turn you blubbering idiot!" On the purple flag I wrote, "Food, gas, lodging, next exit!" On the red flag I wrote, "STOP, in the name of LOVE!" And, on the green flag I wrote, "Straight ahead!"

The flags worked great. It made no difference if my crew was in Shadow flying 70 mph down the highway or if they were sitting still at an intersection, all the crew had to do was hold a flag out the window and I knew exactly what I was supposed to do. When traveling through a congested city, I could spot the brightly colored flag blocks away. Now why couldn't I have thought of that in 2010 when we didn't have the PA system or the headsets?

Team Dex arrived TS9. Flagstaff, Arizona. 536 miles. 52.5 RAAM hours.

RAAM has been described as one crisis after another and Team Dex had seen the truth of this from the very start in Oceanside with the stomach bug that had hit Joni and me, among other, smaller matters. It was only a matter of time, then, before a new big crisis would sneak up on us, and so it was. Elaine had made some delicious salad and pasta, and I was sitting in Bessie at the parking lot of the Flagstaff Mall, cramming down the delicious meal and, at the same time, pleading with pitiful eyes for the ice cream I knew was in the freezer, when Joni and Joe came in to tell me the latest.

When Bessie had been on the alternate route from Congress to Prescott, the crew had heard a loud thunking noise while on a steep climb. Michael investigated and found that the brakes were mushy—not a good thing for the mountainous route that still lay ahead. So, Michael and Conice located a mechanic in Prescott who looked at the brakes and advised them that the rear brakes needed flushing. However, there was no mechanic in Prescott who had the equipment to do the job. Hearing this totally pissed me off because I had Bessie's brakes checked right before departing Del Rio—and we had paid a pretty penny to have the brakes brought up to snuff.

Dan had connections in Flagstaff so he made arrangements for a mechanic shop to look at Bessie. Unfortunately, the shop would not be open until Monday and we were in Flagstaff on a Sunday. So, that is when Dan's friend of nine lives, and Flagstaff resident, Rik Fritz, came to the rescue.

If RAAM is about crisis, it is also about improvising and this latest was simply just a typical crisis that a RAAM crew chief must face. Here was the plan—see if you can keep up with this! Joe's team would stay with Bessie in order to take her to the mechanic the following (Monday) morning. Rik Fritz would drive Dan's team 73 miles ahead along the RAAM route and drop them at a motel in Tuba City, the next time station, where the crew would be able to get a room for a few hours, plus a welcomed shower and rest. The third shift, Conice's team in Shadow, would crew for me as I raced on into Tuba City. Then, in Tuba City, Dan's team would take over follow duties in Shadow while Conice's team would jump out and into the just vacated motel room for their turn at showers and rest. Joe's team would, after Bessie's repairs, then drive to Tuba City and pick up Conice's team. Then those two teams, riding in the RV, would rendezvous—hopefully—in Kayenta, Arizona so Joe's team could relieve Dan's team. At least that was how it was *supposed* to go down.

It was about 8:00 p.m. local time when I departed the Flagstaff Mall and it was here that I first encountered other RAAM racers. Marko Baloh, from Slovenia, flew past me just north of Flagstaff. I had first met Marko, a friend and rival of Jure Robic, at the Texas Hill Country RAAM qualifying race back in March. Marko was one of the favorites to win RAAM 2011.

I also bumped into Dave Elsberry, from Laguna Beach, California. Dave was one of the other 60-year-old racers and he and I rode for a couple of miles together as we departed Flagstaff. (RAAM rules allow riding with other riders for a maximum of 15 minutes per 24 hour period, with no drafting.) Dave was feeling stronger than I was, so eventually he pushed on ahead. David Jones, the other 60+ rider, was already much further ahead of us both.

The first few miles out of Flagstaff were climbing, then the racers dropped from a high elevation of 7200 feet at mile 12 down to 4100 feet at mile 48. The forecast was for 30-40 mph crosswinds from left to right, which initially seemed correct, but then it wasn't long before the sun set on my left and the winds became less cross and more pushing. Dave Elsberry was flying in the winds, but I was too scared to let it all out.

The high winds and the rough road conditions made me nervous. The shoulder was also inconsistent. One minute I had a nice wide shoulder and then all of a sudden there would be no shoulder at all. The traffic was heavy and as soon as it turned nightfall, Shadow went into direct follow and Michael covered my back. Of course it was dark by this time and with the tailwind push, both Shadow and I were moving at a good pace.

Flagstaff to Tuba City was one of the longer time station legs in RAAM at 72 miles and I averaged 23.9 mph with the aid of the favorable winds.

Team Dex arrived TS10. Tuba City, Arizona. 608 miles. 58 RAAM hours.

I felt so sorry for Conice. Not only did he get dumped on at the start of RAAM in Oceanside by being the medic and having to take care of both Joni and myself, but he also had the dubious job of being the bad guy on Team Dex by having to keep track of my off-bike time. He carried a stop watch and would time each and every minute I was off the bike. His job was to constantly remind me that I had been off the bike too long and push me to get back on and ride. Of course, I wanted to stall as long as I could before I had to remount that saddle, so I learned to avoid Conice when I could. I tried my best to make him think my hearing was bad and I couldn't hear a word he was saying. I also avoided eye contact so he wouldn't know I was ignoring him. But Conice is a pretty smart guy and I don't think he bought any of it.

Tuba City is on the Navajo Indian Reservation and the designated time station was the TUUVI Travel Center, which was like a huge convenience store. Dan's crew was waiting at the travel center when we arrived, rested and showered. (Remember? Rik Fritz had brought them ahead since Bessie was sick.) So, there I was, sitting in the navigator's seat in Shadow at the

Travel Center. I had eaten both of the microwave burritos and downed the Dr. Pepper—my favorite drink—Elaine had brought from the store. Then, there was Conice, in my face, tapping his watch on his wrist, telling me, "Dex you've been off your bike 9 minutes. C'mon you need to get going!"

Nine minutes to eat two burritos and drink a Dr. Pepper, and I was wasting time? But Conice was right. So, I mounted that little saddle and I headed off in the dark toward Kayenta, Arizona.

I had departed Tuba City about thirty minutes after midnight local time and became extremely sleepy about 15 miles later. It was dead dark and we were in the middle of the Navajo-Hopi Indian Reservation. I was weaving as I pedaled and was once again experiencing hallucinations. Once, I actually thought I saw a huge 48" plasma TV in the middle of the road. Dan soon decided it was time for a sleep break, so we found a wide spot beside the highway and stopped. Elaine helped me remove my shoes and my helmet and then I crawled up into my little space in the van. By the time my head got to the back of that foam bed, I was dead asleep.

Elaine let me sleep an hour before she was pushing and tugging at me to get up.

Dawn began to break soon after I was back on the road. We were about 20 miles from Kayenta when a RAAM official vehicle passed us then, strangely, stopped right in the middle of the empty highway. I thought to myself, *Now why are they stopping in the middle of the highway? If Team Dex did that we would get slapped with a time penalty!* When I got closer I saw the official was Jim Harms. Jim had been the inspector in Oceanside that had given us the right to race after our pre-race inspection. He was also a big fan of Team Dex in 2010. He was on his way to catch up with the two race leaders, Marko Baloh and Christoph Strasser, but when he saw us, he just had to stop and give his best wishes. Jim will always be one of my favorite RAAM buddies.

Team Dex arrived TS11. Kayenta, Arizona. 679 miles. 66 RAAM hours.

William Richard Perrin: "Dex I'm watching you from Saudi Arabia all day and at only 52 your making me tired just reading about your journey all the time. Good luck!"

Karen Perrin: "Wow! Wow! Wow ! I'm amazed as well. I'm watching from Houston."

Ronnie Early: "Dex—keep on keep'n on. You are doing a great job that many of us armchair bicyclists wish we could do. Thanks for giving us the opportunity to live it through you and to your team for supporting you and keeping us updated. Great job to all of you from Tulsa!!"

Kristin: "Woo hoo! Bring on Utah and it's beautiful scenery!!!! Love you Dex. You're doing awesome!!"

Paul Stanahan: "Dex, I'm checking in on you from CO—very excited to see your progress and cheering for your every pedal stroke. Travel safe and ride like the wind."

Chapter 6

WHERE'S BESSIE?

As I rode into the Mustang Conoco Station in Kayenta, I noticed Caroline van den Bulk's RV in the parking lot. Caroline was one of five females with whom I had started in Oceanside. I wanted to stop and say "Hi", but I had another task weighing heavily on my mind that took immediate priority.

I hurried to the restroom in the store to take a dump, carrying all of my dump supplies with me. Keep in mind that taking a dump wasn't the easiest task at this point. First, I had to remove my double cycling gloves, which wasn't easy because I had lost so much strength in my fingers and hands that I had to use my teeth to get my gloves off. Then I had to pull down two layers of cycling shorts and my short liners. Finally, properly prepared for my duty, I sat on the throne, hoping the urge would come soon so I would have less off-bike time.

After completion of the task, the next step in the process was to put a latex glove on one hand so I could medicate my saddle sores. Given that my coordination was practically zilch at the time, I couldn't get the glove all the way on. I put a small dab of Lanacaine on one finger and blindly reached under my butt hoping that I smeared it on the right spot. Ouch!! Yep, I hit the right spot. After the Lanacaine, my next task was to put some Lantiseptic on my gloved finger and hope that I could smear it over the same spot that I had just smeared with Lanacaine. I also applied Lantiseptic below the front waistline of my shorts to prevent chafing—there is only one thing worse than saddle sores to a male rider and that is Mr. Wiggly sores! Then after all that was completed, I had to carefully pull up and arrange the three layers of shorts, just hoping that I didn't undo everything I had just tediously completed. The entire process took time and my fatigue and loss of coordination made it take even longer and more frustrating. No wonder I had so much off-bike time.

Kalleen Whitford was waiting for me when I came out of the restroom. She is from Dallas, a member of the Lone Star Randonneurs cycling club, and I have known her for years. She was now in RAAM as crew chief for Caroline van den Bulk. Kalleen told me Caroline was sleeping in the RV but, sadly, she also indicated that she thought this was the end of the race for Caroline. Kalleen didn't feel like her racer would continue RAAM once she woke up from her nap.

My heart sank. Whenever I heard of a fellow racer pulling out, I always felt like I had lost a fellow comrade. I know the sacrifice, pain and suffering they have endured, how much courage it takes just to enter RAAM, and I also especially know how much more courage it takes to DNF RAAM.

Caroline's departure would mean that Leah Goldstein and Kathy Roche-Wallace would be the only two remaining of the five females who had started the race. Debbie Tirrito had pulled out at TS7 and Janet Christiansen had stopped at TS5.

It was about 7:30 a.m. local time as I headed out of Kayenta into an absolutely beautiful morning. The temperature was in the mid 60's and the sun was just popping up over some hills on the eastern horizon.

A crew change had been scheduled at Kayenta, but Dan's crew remained in Shadow because we hadn't seen Bessie and gang since we departed Flagstaff. It sure made me wonder if Bessie was still alive. *What if it were to take three or four days to repair Bessie? What if it were a week? What if Bessie had died and had been put to rest in a deserted RV graveyard somewhere on the Navajo Indian Reservation? What if the rest of the crew were on a bus back to Texas? What if Dan, Elaine and Damaris were my only surviving crew? How long could they go on? Could just the four of us make it all the way to Annapolis? Where would they sleep? Would we be getting motel rooms for the remainder of RAAM?* Scary thoughts, these, but the mind wanders like that in RAAM.

Team Dex entered Utah with 700 miles completed and, in keeping with the new tradition, Dan stood on the side of the road as I passed by and yelled out, "Arizona, DONE!"

We were now in Monument Valley and I had never really seen it before. In 2010, it was completely dark when I went through. This year, I was so far behind last year's time, that I would see all its splendor in bright daylight. And, oh my, what a glorious sight! I had seen and admired the John Wayne movie shots taken in Monument Valley but I had no idea how impressive the place would be in person. I was in awe for the next 40 or 50 miles; the scenery was absolutely amazing. Just to see the landmarks of Agathla Peak, Chaistia Butte, Monument Pass, Garden of the Gods and Halchita was something I will always remember.

Shadow was in leapfrog mode and Dan was having an absolute blast photographing the big landscape with the solo cyclist slowly moving through it. It was here that he would take a photo of me going up a big climb with the signature red-rock buttes in the background. This photo would become one of the most recognized and acclaimed photos of my entire RAAM.

Damaris would always be beside the road as I passed, waving that green flag, with a huge smile on her face. Damaris, a beautiful lady with olive-colored skin and the proud mother of two, was the last crew member to sign on to Team Dex. She was born in Panama and her father was in the military so she had traveled the world. She was a fellow teacher of Joni's with the Del Rio school district and, like Em, Damaris had been a 5 O'clock Rocker for years. No matter how hard things were in spin class, I would look over at her and she would be smiling as she spun. It was just a couple of months before RAAM when she approached Em and showed interest in being a crew member. Joni was looking for at least one more and she jumped at the opportunity to add Damaris. Joni and I both met with her and, at the meeting, I tried to paint the bleakest picture of what it would be like to be a RAAM crew member. None of that deterred her, though, and she signed on to Team Dex with no hesitation at all.

There was a nice descent for about the last 10 or 12 miles before we crossed the bridge above the gushing San Juan River leading into Mexican Hat. I was eating well, riding well and putting some time in the bank. Even if I had been racing for over 69 hours, the time was right and the feeling, fine.

Team Dex arrived TS12. Mexican Hat, UT. 724 miles. 70 RAAM hours.

We were still in leapfrog mode as we left Mexican Hat and raced into the Ute Indian Reservation. The nearby hills and mountains were breathtaking, striated with beautiful colors as if an artist had created a multi-layered oil painting. It was absolutely spectacular.

RAAM can play mind games on you, though. The experience is just as much mental as it is physical and you have to keep your head screwed on straight. My thoughts turned to our big, lumbering RV—I still had not heard from Bessie and she should have caught up with us hours ago. *Where was she? Gosh dang it!* I needed to stay mentally strong, but this issue was eating at me.

I finished a seven-mile climb and then had about an 8% grade descent to deal with. I again was overcautious going down and it seemed like the longer I rode, the more exhausted I became and the more confidence I was losing on the descents.

There were several 200' rollers for the first 30 miles heading out of Mexican Hat and Shadow had leapfrogged ahead and was waiting for me somewhere up the road. It was on one of these rollers that all of a sudden I started hearing honking and screaming and yelling coming up from behind. It was Bessie and crew—finally! They came blaring by me, Michael driving and honking, and Joni and Joe hanging out the window screaming, "Go, Dex, go!"

Then, just as fast as they had appeared, they disappeared over the top of the next roller and I was alone again—alone on a two-lane, no-shoulder road out in the middle of the Ute Reservation. There wasn't even a fog line on the pavement. Both Shadow and Bessie were somewhere ahead of me. Of course, true to RAAM, it was then that something happened that I am way too familiar with from my many training miles: my rear wheel went flat. I immediately had to come to a dead stop on the side of the road, with the RAAM clock ticking away. I pulled my cell phone out of my jersey pocket, but there was no service. I looked up and down the road for as far as I could see. Nothing! I listened carefully, but couldn't even hear the roar of a single vehicle. I was definitely stranded.

In our training rides we had practiced leapfrog. I had stressed how it was always better to be behind me than ahead of me. All the crews had practiced staying behind me. However, RAAM requires that support vehicles must remain at least five feet off the shoulder of the road when assisting a rider and that means the vehicle must look for an adequate space to pull out, which can sometimes be difficult to find on certain stretches of road. The crew always knew that if they passed me, it might be several miles before they could find a suitable area to pull over and wait for me. So, that is why it was always better policy to stay behind. The only reason to go ahead of me was when it was time to hand up nutrition or I needed to stop for some reason. Now, I had both vehicles ahead of me precisely when I needed support.

How long would it be before Shadow would notice I wasn't coming? Were Bessie and crew having a reunion party somewhere up the road? Were they celebrating while I was back here stranded? Were they up there talking about the repairs that were done to Bessie?

I know it wasn't that long, but it seemed like forever, when I finally spotted a blue Mazda coming down the road from the opposite direction. I laid my bike in the bar ditch and I walked out in the middle of the road to flag them down. A guy and his wife stopped. I saw the reluctant look on his face as he rolled his window down. I hadn't showered in three days and I was sweaty, stinky and covered in road grime. My skin was leathery from the sun, my mouth had sores, and my tongue was swollen and I could barely talk. I explained to the guy that I was in a "bicycle race across America" and he looked at me like, "Yeah right!" I told him that I had flatted, needed help and that I had a crew up the road. He offered to take me to the crew but I explained to him that it was against the rules for him to give me a ride—again, he just looked at me in bewilderment.

I asked, "Is your cell working?"

He checked and replied, "Yes," then handed me his phone.

I looked at it uncomprehendingly. You see, I don't use smart phones—my personal cell phone is a Wally World pay-as-you-go type. Embarrassed, I handed the phone back to him and asked, "Would you mind calling? I don't know how."

The only phone number I knew was Joni's and luckily, I was able to get in touch with her. Bessie had finally caught up with Shadow on the other side of a long bridge about 1.5 miles up the road from where I had flatted. There was no room for the big RV to pull over so they traveled up the road further to a wider pull-off area. When Joni received my phone call, Bessie immediately turned around and headed my way. As Bessie passed Shadow, Dan was off taking photos and Damaris was standing beside the van. From the RV, Em stuck her head out the window and yelled at Damaris, "He's flatted!"

It wasn't long until I saw Bessie coming back up the road toward me. Of course Bessie didn't have any of my spare wheels, so I still had to wait for Shadow to arrive. Once both crews were there, Dan switched out the rear tubular wheel.

"Gosh dang it!" I was really frustrated. Luckily I had only lost ten minutes, but it could have been so much more if the guy in the Mazda hadn't come along when he did. That is the hazard of leapfrog and having the support vehicle ahead of the rider.

At this point, Joni decided to go ahead and have a crew change. So Conice and crew jumped in Shadow and we were off. The plan was for Bessie to go to the next time station to make me lunch.

Team Dex arrived TS13. Montezuma Creek, UT. 764 miles. 74 RAAM hours

I had flatted about 10 miles short of the next time station, which was in a tiny place called Montezuma Creek. Once we were back on the road after the wheel and crew change, I started complaining to Conice about being hungry—poor Conice, he always gets the complaints. Conice told me that Joni was planning a food stop for me at Montezuma Creek.

Just before the time station, there was an "S" curve and a set of railroad tracks. Conice wanted to be certain that I made it through this tricky section, so Shadow, in leapfrog mode, was pulled over to the side of the curve waiting to signal me. I made it across the railroad tracks safely and immediately after that I looked over and saw Bessie filling up with gas at a small Texaco gas station. No one around Bessie indicated anything to me so I just kept pedaling.

Once Shadow caught up with me, Conice informed me that the gas station had been the time station—I had just missed my food. Now I was not only hungry, I was also pissed. So what's new? Thankfully, Shadow had a little 200-watt rice cooker in it, so Anika heated up some cheese on a round piece of bread. It was really good. In fact, it was so good that I asked, "Anika, will you please make me another one of those delicious cheese sandwiches?"

She looked at me with her big brown eyes as if she knew how sarcastic I was being, then just as sarcastically, she replied, "Of course, kind sir."

I was serious, though, I was starving and they tasted really good!

We were still following the San Juan River as we left Montezuma Creek and started toward Cortez, Colorado. It wasn't long before we left the state highway and began following ranch roads around Ute Mountain—and I do mean ranch roads. The road was nothing more than loose gravel and dirt. Every time a rancher driving his dually 4-wheel drive monster truck would meet me, the dust his truck kicked up would suffocate me.

Shadow continued in leapfrog mode and, at some point on the gravel road, I saw Anika standing by the parked van and as I passed she yelled, "Utah, DONE!"

I had no idea I was crossing into Colorado as there was no sign or state marker that I saw.

But the rough, gravel road continued on. "Gosh dang it!" I was really pissed. *What was George, the RAAM race director, thinking? Colorado is his home state! You would think he would want good roads in his own home state! That darn George! I can't wait until I see him again! I'm going to tell him off! Gosh dang it!* I started taking more and more breaks—stopping for a pee, stopping to eat, stopping for this and stopping for that. I was becoming an expert procrastinator and I was accumulating a lot of off-bike time on this section.

I eventually started taking the terrible road conditions out on my crew. Each time I would pass them as they were parked on the side of the road, I would yell, "How much further on this stuff?" Poor Anika wouldn't say a word. She would just lower her head like she was so sorry but there was nothing she could do about it.

Michael would yell, "You don't worry about it and just keep riding!"

Conice just said, "You are doing great. Keep going!"

I was complaining to them and talking to myself. *It wasn't their fault but it sure as hell wasn't mine, so why shouldn't I blame it on them?*

About then, I looked up the road and could see the flashing tail lights of another RAAM support vehicle parked off of the road, a dark blue van with a back-up bike on the roof and the number 415 on the rear gate. As I passed, I looked at the signage on the door and it said Kathy-Roche Wallace. There was a young man in the driver's seat and another even younger male navigating. As I rounded a sharp curve I saw Kathy riding ahead, so I pulled up beside her. She didn't appear to be in any better frame of mind than I was. The gravel road sucked. We didn't introduce ourselves as neither of us was exactly in a social mood at the time. I did ask her how it was going, though, and she replied, "I have bad saddle sores."

I noticed as we rode that she was wearing her cycling shorts inside out—she was trying anything she could think of to minimize the pain.

She stood on her pedals most of the time she rode and when she wasn't standing, she wouldn't sit directly on her saddle. Instead, she would lean to one side and rest her weight on her quad across the top tube of the bike.

It is a RAAM rule that you can't draft off of another rider. You can ride beside another rider, but only for 15 minutes per 24 hours, so I slowly went on ahead of Kathy. It wasn't long before her support crew passed us both and pulled off to the side of the road again to wait for her. As I passed, I yelled at the young man, "How much further on this gravel?" *I might as well take it out on him, too.*

Kathy and I kept yo-yoing back and forth and we would talk briefly as we passed each other. She was really hurting. She had been way ahead of me but she had slowed as her sores worsened. She indicated to me she was really worried about making the 87 hour mandatory cut-off time at Durango.

Kathy's condition got me to thinking about Joni's secret treatment for saddle sores—Lanacaine spray, Lantiseptic, Neosporin and Dermoplast Spray, all applied in a special sequence. Her remedy won't cure saddle sores but it will sure keep them intact and prevent them from worsening. So, I told my crew to call up ahead to Bessie and have Joni share some of our saddle sore supplies and recipe with Kathy's crew chief.

Having another racer and crew nearby on the course helped me pass some of the miles. When Kathy was ahead of me, she was like a carrot; when she was behind, she was like a chasing hound. I would talk to her crew each time I passed—they were both cool kids. Finally though, there came a time when Kathy stopped and I kept going. I would look over my shoulder to see if she was still following but she wasn't there. I felt sad. I imagined that was the last time I would ever see her. Our paths had crossed ever so briefly—two people sharing something so rare, so unique.

I finally hit US 160 and got onto a real, paved road, although the route was continually climbing by this time. We would eventually reach 6200 feet of elevation before arriving in Cortez. About 10 miles before Cortez, another RAAM rider passed me. I was on a steep climb at the time and the guy came around me effortlessly. I didn't recognize who he was but since I knew that Marko Baloh and Christoph Strasser were the only two males ahead of me, whoever this guy was had to be the third place male overall at this point. It was kind of embarrassing to have a guy that started 24 hours later than you pass you within the first 800 miles of the race.

My next encounter with another RAAM racer was just past a long bridge where I could see a support vehicle parked. When the rider ahead stopped to grab some food I pulled over. The rider was Mark Pattison, a strong RAAM veteran from Westport, Connecticut. He was looking great. We wished each other well and parted ways. As he pulled on ahead I knew I would never see him again until the finish.

Team Dex arrived TS14. Cortez, CO. 814 miles. 79 RAAM hours.

Upon leaving Cortez, Team Dex entered the heart of the Rockies where the RAAM route book warned us about the traffic: "The route is now getting into the serious climbing of the Rocky Mountains. Here live some of the best, most skilled and fastest automobile drivers in the country. At night they will see your unusual lights and perhaps give you extra room while wondering what you are up to. But, at dusk, dawn and during rush hours they are less likely to see you before blowing by too close for comfort. CREWS PROTECT YOUR RACERS!"

Well, the route book was right about crews needing to protect their racers. Joe and crew were now in Shadow, it was night and we had gone to direct follow mode. US 160 was like a high speed freeway and all I could see ahead of me were the headlights and taillights of a constant stream of motorists. Joe kept trying to play my music on the speakers but the noise of the cars zooming by was so loud that I couldn't hear it. I kept complaining to Joe through the headset about the traffic—as if he could do anything about it!

I was nervous and scared. The road would climb for a couple of miles then I would descend for a couple of miles. I was really fearful on the descents, especially at night with the cars zooming so closely by. I began to wish I were back on that secluded gravel road!

Finally, after about 1:00 a.m., the traffic lightened up and I felt a little more comfortable, helped by Em who talked to me over the headset while she drove, trying to reassure me. Em lives an extremely busy life as a loving mother of two young boys and with a professional career as a financial advisor. Passionate and energetic about everything she pursues, she is an active member of the Rotary Club as well as several other civic organizations. There probably aren't many community committees in Del

Rio that she doesn't chair. Em has to be one of the most unselfish people I know.

I first met Em about three years ago. She was a die-hard 5 O'clock Rocker—even with her busy life, she never missed the 5:00 a.m. class. She didn't just come to spin class to merely ride the bike for an hour—she attacked the bike. Her competitive edge was obvious. In spin class, I would put on a hard song like Guns-N-Roses' *Paradise City*, then I would move my spin bike directly in front of and just inches away from Em. We would be facing each other, going one on one, challenging each other to push it harder and harder.

Em and I became close friends and she was the one person I wanted on my crew in 2010 but she just wasn't able to pull it off. When the 2010 race started, she became obsessed with tracking my progress. She was constantly online or on the phone talking to others, attempting to get more updates. She was so caught up in following my RAAM that year that she actually broke out in an itchy red rash all over her arms. The rash didn't disappear until RAAM was over.

When I finally decided that I was going to return to RAAM in 2011, Em was the very first crew member Joni sought. She and her husband Bill thought and prayed about it. She had to consider her boys, her business and her already booked vacation to Africa. Bill supported her and she agreed to make the sacrifice to join the crew. Not only did she join the crew, but she also spearheaded the fundraising campaign for BCFS, dedicating hours of work to the Evening With Dex party. She was always looking for ways to do more for Team Dex.

Now, with Em watching the reality of the performance, I felt embarrassed and revealed for who I truly was. Before RAAM, I felt like, in her mind, she had always seen me as some kind of super hero as if she held me up on a pedestal above others—and now that she was actually seeing me in real life, I wasn't living up to her expectations. She was seeing the RAAM Dex. She was seeing just a regular guy that rides his bike very slowly and complains about everything. She was seeing a coward that couldn't ride down a hill without getting terrified.

I struggled up yet another, longer climb to the summit of Hesperus Hill, then started down a marked 6% descent for about the next eight miles. I was terrified. It was dark and it was difficult to see the road as I went down the hill. It was cold, too, which contributed to my shivering and making the bike a bit unstable, so I kept feathering my brakes. I was getting pissed off at myself. Any other rider would be putting time in the bank on these descents, yet they were costing me time. I was embarrassed that Em was seeing me this way. I felt like such a coward.

Total exhaustion and sleep deprivation affect people differently. It affects me not only negatively but also makes me a bit paranoid. I was at a mental low and I arrived in Durango nine hours slower than I did in 2010 which just fed into my negativity and paranoia. *How in the world was I going to finish RAAM?*

TS15 was at Gateway Park in Durango and all crews were required to call into the RAAM War Room before arrival to find out if they had any time penalties. If so, they had to stop to serve out their sentence. Luckily, Team Dex didn't have any penalties so we would be able to keep going. Most critically for me, TS15 was also the first of three mandatory time cut-off stations—I had to arrive in less than 87 RAAM hours to keep from being disqualified from the race. I made it, but by less than 2 ½ hours.

Team Dex arrived TS15. Durango CO. 857 miles.
84 hours 36 minutes.

No Show and Michelle: "Dex and Team, it was truly an inspiration to see you all in action the other night. Last year, we followed you all the way to the end. It was a straight shot of reality seeing the rhythmic motions of you and your team. Just know that we were honored to have the opportunity to be in the direct presence of a hero. You and your team exemplify the true meaning of determination. Aidan, my five-year-old asks about you all the time. He says that when he grows up, he is going to Race Across America. God Bless you and your team."

Jackie and Johnny: "Go, Dex, Go! May you always ride where the rain don't hit ya, where the snakes don't crawl, and the bears don't get ya!"

Jim Burr: "Great going. Hang in there for all us older guys."

Lisa Bliss: "Way to go Team Dex for getting our guy to Durango safe and beating the 6 a.m. cut-off."

Kyndle: "Yeah!!!!! GO, TEAM DEX, GO . . . GO!!! Uncle Dexter, you're a machine! Absolutely awesome job!!! This is YOUR race, you OWN it!!! Love you!!!"

Chapter 7

WOLF CREEK, LA VETA AND CUCHARA

I had heard from more than just a few RAAM experts that racers should not use family, especially their spouse, as crew members on RAAM. The reason given is usually that family members have a tendency to be soft. They are more likely to be compromising with the racer and they often lack the required sternness. In short, when they see their loved one in such pain and exhaustion, they are more likely to act with their heart and less likely to keep pushing the racer beyond their limits. Well, all I can say is that those people have never met my wife, Joni. You can accuse Joni of many things, but being soft is not one of them.

Joni is much like Rene Russo's character, Molly Griswold, from the movie *Tincup*. In the movie, Molly's role is girlfriend and psychiatrist to Roy McAvoy, played by Kevin Costner. Roy is a failed pro golfer whose talents are good enough to qualify him for the U. S. Open. During the golf tournament of his life, the key scene of the film, Roy is in the hunt for the Open Championship as he approaches the par five final hole, a hole with a water hazard protecting the green. After hitting the fairway with his drive, the prudent safe shot is to take a seven iron and lay it up. But Roy has the inability to resist a dare or a challenge, so he elects to go for the green and ends up hitting the ball into the water. He could still make par from the drop zone, but instead of playing it safe, Roy elects to hit his ball from the same spot just to prove he can make the shot. But, he doesn't make it and he repeatedly hits balls into the water. Fellow golf pros, fans in the crowd and TV announcers watch in total disbelief as Roy's U. S. Open hopes and dreams are literally drowned. Roy continues to hit balls into the water until he is down to the last ball in his bag. If Roy hits this ball into the brink, then he will be disqualified from the Open. While everyone else says no, don't do it, Molly understands his crazy need to push beyond the ordinary and prove to everyone that he can make the shot. While she stands in the crowd laughing to herself and thinking he's crazy, she still yells encouragement to Roy, "Oh God, Roy, you're right! Go for it, Roy! Just knock it on! Let'er rip!"

When Roy finally hits his final ball onto the green, Molly yells in support, "Oh Roy, I love you! In five years no one will remember who won the U. S. Open but nobody will ever forget your 12 on that last hole!"

Joni is Molly. She isn't going to give an inch. She will push me and support me regardless of my crazy antics and risks. She knows how much I want to prove I can do this. No, Joni is definitely not soft!

I went down for a sleep as soon as I arrived in Durango at TS15. Bessie, with a nice memory-foam, queen-sized bed, was right there waiting, but Joni had Anika blocking the door to Bessie. Instead of getting to sleep in the comfort of Bessie, Joni directed me back to Shadow explaining that Bessie was off limits to me. When I questioned why, she just said, "Because I am crew chief and I say so!" No, she definitely is not soft!

I removed my helmet and cycling shoes. My road grime-stained shorts and jersey remained on. It was cold in the van as I crawled up into the tiny space where my luxurious piece of foam called a bed lay. Anika covered me with a blanket and I was out like a light. Joni let me sleep the shortest two hours of my life.

It was still dark when I awoke. Joni got me up and helped me walk over to Bessie as if she were helping a staggering drunk across the street. She tried to coax me to walk faster by telling me Elaine had some breakfast ready. *At least she was going to let me eat.*

It was then I noticed a small crowd of people standing near Bessie. Some of them were wrapped in blankets trying to stay warm while others had cameras and video equipment. Joni scurried me past the small crowd and into Bessie. Elaine had delicious scrambled eggs with lots of cheddar cheese ready for me. I ate three helpings and drank some pink-looking Vitamin Water. I was dead tired and also extremely confused. While Joni was medicating my butt I kept hearing my name being mentioned by the people outside Bessie.

I asked Joni, "Where am I? What is going on? Who are those people outside?"

Joni saw the blank look on my face and immediately understood I really didn't have any idea what was going on—she had seen me go through this same thing in 2010. She replied, "You are in a bicycle race. The race is called RAAM. The people outside are media people. They want to interview you and take your photo. One of Joe's friends from El Paso, Chris and his wife, are also out there. They came to see you."

I just stared at Joni and asked, "RAAM?"

Joni replied, "Babe, you just need to get on your bike and ride."

Elaine was standing in the kitchen listening and watching. She told me later that she had tears in her eyes—she had never seen a person, especially a friend like me, in such a dazed and confused state. She felt so helpless, thinking to herself, *How in the world is he doing this? This is frigging scary! What am I doing here?* She texted her husband and son to tell them how upsetting this was: "Dex is so out of it. He'll never make it. This race is crazy." Then, thinking better of it, she erased the text.

I stepped out of Bessie only to find bright camera lights shining on me illuminating the dark night. I heard people asking questions, but Joe and Joni were guiding me toward my bike; there wasn't time for interviews. I looked into the crowd and saw Joe's friend, Chris. I thought to myself, *Here it is, not even sunrise yet, and this guy and his wife are standing out here in the cold with blankets wrapped around themselves just to see me for two minutes and say Hi.*

I mounted my bike, Damaris turned my bike lights on, Anika turned my helmet light on, and Dan gave me directions on how to exit the time station. Joe and crew were already in Shadow waiting to drop in behind me. As I clipped into my pedals I called out, "Hey Chris, thanks for coming out. I didn't expect to see you here."

Joe cranked up ZZ Top's *La Grange* on Shadow's speakers and I was off into the black night.

I was now heading east to Pagosa Springs. I liked the word "east." It was very important to me to always be heading east. I still had over 2000 more eastern miles to go and we were headed toward some very challenging Rocky Mountain passes. From here, the climb to the Continental Divide would begin.

The sky began to lighten and the sun finally came up so, with daylight, Shadow reverted to leapfrog mode. A bit later, Palo Asti, the racer from Italy that I had met on the Sunday pre-ride, came up to me on the nine-mile climb up Baldy Mountain. The combination of the language barrier and the steep climb in such thin air made it difficult to talk, though, so we just smiled at each other.

Along this section of the course were pretty valleys filled with horses grazing in pastures. I have always had a penchant and knack for talking with horses as I ride—so much so that a friend, Ryan Van Duzer, calls me "the horse whisperer." When I talk to them, the horses become alert and turn to face me directly, with questions in their eyes. I detect their bewilderment about why this crazy-looking human in a bright-colored jersey and spandex shorts was pedaling that weird-looking, two-wheeled contraption down the road. I just stare back at them and call out, "Horsey.... Horsey.... Horsey.... C'mon Horsey.... Talk to me!"

It was a beautiful Rocky Mountain morning, which got me to pondering some of the music written about these high peaks. I know I would be shot if any Colorado locals heard me say this, but I cannot stand John Denver. His songs sound so cheesy to me—and Em knew this. So, the next time I passed her on the side of the road, just to piss me off, she had *Rocky Mountain High* playing on Shadow's sound system. I immediately got nauseous, and it wasn't the altitude.

Team Dex arrived TS16. Pagosa Springs, CO. 912 miles. 92 RAAM hours.

Conice's crew came on duty in Shadow as we got closer to the famous Wolf Creek Pass. Months before RAAM, Conice had requested of Joni that he be in Shadow as I climbed Wolf Creek—he and his family had vacationed here for years and he knew this area of Colorado well. Well, Conice got his wish.

About four miles outside of Pagosa Springs, a local cyclist met up with me on the road. I could tell he was a hammerhead from his skin tight jersey and bibs. He was riding a Trek Madone with the newest, lightest, fastest Dura Ace components and was on a training ride that included Wolf Creek Pass. He didn't even introduce himself before he started bragging about his thousand-dollar Power Tap watt-monitoring system and his new training program from his online personal coach. After learning I was in RAAM, he immediately started talking about how he planned on doing RAAM one day. He told me he was going to do it this year but one thing or another got in his way. I was so tired and exhausted I wasn't hearing half of what he was bragging about.

There are RAAM talkers and then there are RAAM doers, and this guy was definitely a talker. It floors me how cyclists are constantly not only telling me how they could do RAAM, but also telling me how *I* should do RAAM. They can all do it on paper, of course. They get out their little calculator and they divide miles by hours and figure out all they have to do is average 10 mph. Then they tell me that if they were doing RAAM, they would do it this way or that way. They have no clue. Sure, any cyclist can average 10 mph for one day, but can he or she average 10 mph for 12 consecutive days? Can she average 10 mph in her sleep? True, it does work out to about a 10 mph average—that is, if you don't ever once stop during those twelve days to eat, pee, change a wheel or sleep. These riders have all kinds of advice for me about ultra racing when most of them don't do but a half-dozen century rides a year and most have never done a double century. They understand RAAM on paper, but they have no idea of the harsh reality of it. The race isn't just about the daily miles, total miles or average speed. RAAM is about having the passion in your soul to dig down deep and push on when you are at and beyond your physical and emotional limits. It isn't about riding with your legs; RAAM is about riding with your heart.

I quickly got tired of his advice, so I told him that RAAM rules prohibited me from riding with other riders and I hoped he had a good climb up Wolf Creek. He understood. He grabbed a couple of gears, stood up on his pedals and sped on away from me. Then, after just a short distance, he turned around to look back at me just to see if I had been impressed with his sudden burst of power. *Typical hammerhead!*

Soon, I was nearing the start of the actual climb up to Wolf Creek Pass. At one point, to keep me on course, Anika was on the side of the road letting me know I needed to bear left ahead. Then I saw several cars parked along the shoulder of the road. It seemed odd to me to see people standing outside their cars holding signs but, to my complete surprise, I quickly realized that it was Tommy and Jowanna Griffin, friends from my home town of Crane, Texas. They were visiting the Wolf Creek area and had been following me online. It really meant a lot to me to see some Crane folks as I started the climb.

Starting with the 2010 RAAM, fans—like my friends from Crane—who followed me became known as Dexans, a witty merge of my name with the name of my home state. Just why this movement started was an interesting question, since I was new to the ultra scene, wasn't a big name athlete, and I had never been associated with RAAM.

While we live in a day and age when professional athletes are often associated with performance enhancing drugs, sex scandals and violence, I think the Dexan movement began with the idea that I was just "the guy next door" who people could identify with. I think I represented a fresh breath of air to everyday people all over the world who were tired of the typical sports athlete. For the two weeks of RAAM, people could put aside the arrogance of today's trash-talking super athletes and their million-dollar contracts and connect with an ordinary guy chasing his dream of achieving the extraordinary. I was the storybook underdog chasing his dream under the most difficult circumstances.

In 2010, Dexans watched via internet as I left California on the seemingly impossible task of crossing the United States on a bicycle in 12 days at the age of 60. They followed me through the intense heat of the Mojave Desert and the wind and rain of the Rockies. News of my challenge spread quickly through the electronic airways and my website began to collect hits from all across the nation and around the world. They saw my never-say-die attitude as I hit the unprecedented high winds, cold weather and torrential thunderstorms in Colorado. They would wake up in the middle of the night unable to resist going to their computer to check the website just to see if "he" was still riding. They watched as I fought the flood waters in Kansas. They would sneak online at work just to read the updates posted by my webmaster and crew that described the injuries, pain, delirium and sleep deprivation I was experiencing. Fans were complaining because they weren't getting updates soon enough. They sat on the edge of their chairs in front of their computer screens and sent electronic comments and cheers as I barely made the Mississippi River mandatory cut-off time limit. Hundreds if not thousands of Dexans vicariously rode with me those final hours of RAAM 2010. They watched as I refused to give up. And they cried when I finally surrendered in Maryland due to time restrictions, just 180 miles from that finish line.

In 2011, the Dexan addiction continued unabated and, to help them out, we introduced a new tracking device. My boss, Mike Wrob, set up a web link with a GPS tracking device so fans could track me live at any time all the way from Oceanside to Annapolis. Mauro Faz, the IT person at Marathon Heater installed the tracking device in Shadow. The only problem we had with it was that the crew had to remember to reset the device every 24 hours or it would automatically quit tracking—and this happened every now and then.

So, there I was at the foot of Wolf Creek Pass, the signature climb of RAAM. The sign gave me the distance: "Summit 8 miles." For these next eight miles I would be climbing a 7% grade up to a final elevation of over two miles above sea level. The thin, dry air at 10,857 feet had ended RAAM for several racers during past years. Many developed severe respiratory complications, including pneumonia. In 2006, Jure Robic was leading RAAM when he went through Pagosa Springs, but his race ended at the summit of Wolf Creek Pass when he was airlifted to a medical facility due to respiratory problems.

I climbed slowly. I was struggling. Even though I had a tailwind push, I was really having a hard time. I was in my lowest gear and I just kept slowly working up the climb, gasping for air. I would stand on my pedals and climb, then I would sit down on my saddle for a while. Climbing was normally my forte—but not that day.

Conice, Michael and Anika would leapfrog ahead in Shadow and cheer me on with encouragement as I passed. This was Michael's first time in Colorado and he was amazed at the majesty of the San Juan Mountains. He was obviously in good spirits as he and Conice tossed snowballs at each other.

I have known Michael for several years. He is one of the IT guys at Marathon Heater and is a co-worker of mine. Our cubicles are next to each other so we see each other's ugly faces daily. A dedicated husband, he is also the father of two young boys.

I wanted Michael on the 2010 crew but there was just no way he could break away from his family for two weeks while he gallivanted across the nation following some idiot on a bicycle. When I returned to work in 2010, following RAAM, it became very apparent to me just how much RAAM meant to Michael. Out of nowhere he came up to me and gave me the biggest, hardest, emotion-filled unmanly hug I have ever received. So when I finally decided I was going to try RAAM again in 2011, I made sure Michael was one of the first potential crew members that Joni contacted. To my utter pleasure, Michael said yes to being a part of my crazy venture. He admitted he had wanted to go in 2010 but it just didn't work out. This time his wife, Flora, insisted that he go.

Michael is a very capable young man with some serious technology savvy. Even as early as January he was helping me keep my website updated. He was instrumental in many of the pre-RAAM preparations, spending countless hours working on Bessie and preparing her for another 6000-mile odyssey. He was the one who guided Joni in finding the wireless microphone system that solved our communication problems. Anytime Joni needed any assistance with preparing the van or the RV for our 2011 venture, he was right there. When she ran into problems working on the RV, he was quick to help out. So, Michael quickly and naturally became the MacGyver of Team Dex. Even if he didn't have the right tools, he could fix anything—he would contrive *something* to make it work. He became our go-to guy anytime we struggled with solving a problem, and Michael usually came up with the answer.

Early on, Michael signed up for several of the long, extended training rides and even crewed for me on the Texas Hill Country 600 race. Joni soon found that he was an excellent driver—he could stay behind the wheel for extended periods of time without falling asleep. I guess being a father of two very young boys must have helped him develop that skill!

Michael was determined to help me reach my goal of finishing RAAM in 2011. I think he, more than any other crew member, realized how critical his help would be in getting me across that finish line and he never once took it lightly. He had no pre-conceptions this was going to be any kind of vacation. While other crew members were excited and looked forward to RAAM as an adventure, Michael kept focused and looked at crewing RAAM as a job. A job he took very seriously. I was very lucky to have a crew member like Michael.

I finally made it to the summit of Wolf Creek. Conice and the Shadow crew were waiting for me, and Bessie and the rest of the crew arrived within five minutes. We asked a nearby tourist to take a Team Dex group shot in front of the sign marking The Great Divide.

As important as the Continental Divide milestone was, in a way, all of this was anticlimactic for me. In 2010, I had a very strong climb up Wolf Creek. In fact, in 2010, my time split up Wolf Creek Pass was faster than most other RAAM racers, including Jure.

When I had reached the summit in 2010, it was almost like an epiphany for me. At the time, Joe, Eldon and Merry were in Shadow in direct follow while Bessie and crew were already waiting for me at the top. As we neared the summit, Joe began playing Joni's and my favorite song, *One Day* by Matisyahu. Joni could hear the song as I came closer. Time seemed to stand still just for a moment as I looked ahead and saw

Joni standing in the road. My emotions overtook me and I began sobbing out loud with huge tears running down from my eyes. I stood up on my pedals and I began sprinting up the final yards of Wolf Creek. I kept yelling "Joni, Joni, Joni!" She began to run toward me. It was just like the classic movie scene of two young lovers running toward each other in slow motion on a beach. As I got closer to Joni I could see her tears of joy and love. This was a moment neither of us will ever forget.

Mark, Lisa and Raul were caught up in the emotion as well as they ran to meet us. The entire Team cried and hugged. The spirit and enormity of RAAM had captured us all atop Wolf Creek Pass.

But, that was 2010 and this was 2011. I should have known there was no way I could expect the same electric moment.

Now, summit photo recorded, I had to face the horrifying descent—twenty miles of steep, curvy road in gusty winds lay ahead. Since I knew I would be scared, I asked Conice to keep Shadow well behind me as I went down. Once again, at a time when other racers would use the descent to recover from their hard climbing efforts, I was tense and terrified. I concentrated and tried to focus on the task—I needed to get down the mountain without having one of my bike seizures. I didn't care how slow I went or how long it took me, I just knew I could not afford to crash and end my RAAM. *What a terrible attitude to have to deal with. Why couldn't I just get over this head thing? I am a grown man. I am an accomplished rider. I have been doing this stuff for decades. Why can't I conquer this fear? Gosh dang it!*

Team Dex arrived TS17. South Fork, CO. 960 miles. 97.5 RAAM hours.

South Fork was the beginning of my demise in 2010 as it was where the 40-60 mph winds first hit me, but this year I had a good tail/cross wind as I headed toward Alamosa—this was my opportunity to put some time in the bank. Dan's crew was now on duty and in leapfrog mode. The Rio Grande River, the river I live less than a half-mile from, well to the south in Del Rio, Texas, was just out of my sight to the left.

My appetite remained good. I was doing a good job of downing my 200-calorie flasks every hour, and, of course, I was scarfing down every bit of solid food I could get my hands on when I was stopped. The combination of the liquid diet and having my mouth gaped open for about the last 100 hours straight had led to sores in my mouth and on my tongue. My tongue was swollen to the point that it was difficult for me to speak. I preferred to eat with plastic forks and spoons because metallic utensils aggravated my mouth sores. Elaine offered me some WOW oral rinse to help out.

Elaine was a surprise member to Team Dex. In November of 2010, Joni and I had sent out an announcement to start attempting to assemble a crew. We called a meeting at our house and invited anyone that thought they were crazy enough or willing enough to crew RAAM. I didn't know Elaine at that time, at least not very well, but I did know there was no doubt about her enthusiasm when she had followed me in the 2010 RAAM, so I sent her a last minute email inviting her to the meeting.

Elaine has RV knowledge and loves to camp out, so the rigors of RAAM crew life would not be a problem, but more importantly she loves to take care of others. She is married and has a grown son, so we felt she might be available to leave her responsibilities for the twelve-day journey. Oh yeah, one other thing Elaine can do . . . . COOK! She is an awesome cook. I benefited from her expertise throughout my whole RAAM experience.

Elaine proved to be one of the most important crew members in other ways, too. Her cheerful, jovial personality kept things light among the crew. She was such a delight and just the type of person that makes you want to spend time with her. She committed to more training rides than any other crew member, and was jealous when Joni had to train others. This made her the most prepared of the crew members and that proved to be very important during RAAM 2011. Joni relied on her more than any of the others because she knew Elaine was confident, trained, and knew exactly what to do. Then there was also that kindred spirit thing going on between them as Elaine is a retired teacher and that fact alone was enough for Joni to have great confidence in her. Since Joni is also a teacher, she recognizes specific strengths in people and she has told me many times, "Teachers naturally get along with others and are more forgiving and understanding than many people. Teachers also are willing to do whatever has to be done to get the job done. We're trained to be that way." Joni's insight about teachers turned out to be exactly right, especially in Elaine's case.

Team Dex arrived TS18. Alamosa, CO. 1006 miles. 100 RAAM hours.

It was dark as Joe's crew took over in Shadow in direct follow mode and I made the best of the continuing tailwind for about the next 30 miles. Then, just as I started my assault up La Veta Pass, Joe told me through the headset that another RAAM rider was approaching. It was Joshua Kench, from New Zealand. Joshua and crew had been staying at the same hotel as Team Dex in Oceanside and I had attempted to talk with him there but, between his thick New Zealand accent and my West Texas twang, neither one of us understood very well what the other was saying.

Now he rode up beside me and I asked him, "How's it goin'?"

I could tell from the way he looked at me that he didn't understand what I had asked. But being the gentleman he was, he smiled and replied back something to me which I didn't understand either. I had to laugh to myself about what was taking place. Here were two guys from two different continents, both having raced over 1000 non-stop miles on a bicycle. Our minds and our bodies were mush—we couldn't even keep our own thoughts straight—and even though we were both speaking English, neither had any idea what the other was saying.

So, just for the hell of it, knowing Josh wouldn't have any idea what I was saying, I said to him, "My crew has a six-pack of beer and a cheeseburger with curly fries, want some?"

Joshua smiled courteously and replied with something but I had no idea what. He then gave me a friendly hand gesture to indicate he was going ahead. We wished each other luck and safety. Neither of us needed to understand the words, but both of us felt the camaraderie of RAAM.

La Veta Pass kicked my butt in 2010. That year, there was high wind, lightening, small hail and cold rain. I was eventually overcome by hyperthermia and had to be pulled off the course to be warmed up. La Veta was the demise of my RAAM in 2010 and so the nightmare of it all returned to my mind as I headed up the climb.

The weather was 100% better this year—the winds were tolerable and the temperature was in the low 50's. I even worked up a sweat as I made my way up the 6% grade. Em was doing a good job of keeping me in the headlight beams as we snaked around the switchback curves. Joe was playing Joe Cocker's *With a Little Help from My Friends* on the sound system. It gave me inspiration on the climb as I thought back to my spin class and all the Rockers.

I crested the top and immediately started a four-mile descent into the village of La Veta. My jersey was wet from the climb, though, and I soon became chilled on the descent and I started shivering beyond control. I told Joe I needed to stop to get warm. La Veta was doing it again—she was kicking my butt just like in 2010.

I was just a couple of miles from the time station when Em finally found a wide spot on the road where we could pull over. Joni placed me in the navigator's seat in Shadow where the heater could get me warm. She wrapped a blanket around me. I sat shivering for about five or ten minutes until I finally warmed up enough that I was able to get back on my bike and make it to the TS.

Team Dex arrived TS19. La Veta, CO. 1064 miles. 106 RAAM hours.

Upon arrival at the time station, I was dead tired, delirious and cold. I needed to go down for a sleep. I sat like an invalid in the domestique's seat while Joni removed my helmet and shoes. She told me I had to sleep in Shadow—Bessie was there, but off-limits. She helped me change into a dry undershirt and long sleeve jersey. I crawled up into my little space, Joni covered me with a blanket and I slept for 60 minutes. It seemed like no time at all before Joni was pushing on my butt saying, "Got to get up, Babe. It's time to go."

Through my sleepy haze, I mumbled, "What?"

"Time to ride your bike, Babe. We have breakfast ready."

Elaine had made a couple of egg burritos with bacon and lot of cheese. I normally don't eat meat with breakfast but I couldn't get enough of that bacon. I departed La Veta in the cold night at about 1:00 a.m. local time. I had it in my mind that the climb out of La Veta up to Cuchara Pass was extremely steep but no longer than two or three miles, then I would start a gradual descent all the way to Trinidad—boy, was I wrong!

Conice and crew were back in Shadow and Michael, in his spot behind the wheel, would have his work cut out for him trying to keep me in the headlights on the narrow, curvy climb. I started the steep ascent up Cuchara, but I was so exhausted and the grade so steep that I needed at least a couple of more teeth on my rear cassette. I started zigzagging back and forth across the road just to make it up the steeper grades. I was delirious and kept telling myself, *Just don't stop. If you stop, you will never be able to clip back into your pedals on this steep grade. Don't stop. Keep climbing. This is only a three-mile climb. I've probably already climbed a mile of it so that means there are only two miles left. Just don't stop.*

I didn't stop, but neither did the climb—and by then I knew I had gone farther than three miles. I kept zigzagging to keep my upward momentum and the narrow road kept snaking its way uphill. All I could see was what was in the headlight beam in front of me and each time I would round a curve, I would think, *This has got to be the last curve. I know the summit is right here. It has to be. I know I have gone further than three miles.*

Conice told me another rider was coming up and that Michael would be slowing so as to allow the rider and their follow vehicle to pass. The rider was Bachman Hermann, from Switzerland. Bachman was the RAAM leader in the 50+ age group and he and his crew passed me as if I were standing still.

I continued up and up and up. *I know I have climbed five or six miles now. Where the hell is that summit?* I was getting very mentally frustrated. I dug deep and just kept pushing, knowing I could not give in to the mental frustration. RAAM is all about attitude and I knew if I ever gave in, it would break me. Once RAAM breaks you, it is over.

I screamed out loud on each steep grade, "AHHHHHHH, AHHHHHHHH!" Conice, on the headset, was getting an earful. *Gosh dang it!* I had been so wrong. What I had in my mind as a three-mile climb was actually an 18-mile climb. I thought it was never going to end. For me, it would end up being one of the toughest and most crucial stages in RAAM.

When we finally reached the summit, we saw Bachman and team pulled over on the side of the road and it appeared he was putting on warm clothing for the descent. We would later learn, however, that the leader of the 50+ age group actually DNFed at the summit of La Veta. I had no idea what happened. Maybe RAAM had broken his attitude.

Then, as dawn approached, I started the gradual descent toward Trinidad. The climb up to Cuchara Pass had completely zapped me, though, and I couldn't stay awake and was weaving back and forth across the road. There was one moment when I thought I saw an ex-high school classmate run across the road in front of me and I swerved to miss her.

Conice and Michael decided that even though it had only been a few hours since La Veta where I had slept, they would put me down again.

I went down in Shadow for a 30-minute nap and it was the break of dawn when they got me up. Anika gave me a Balance Bar, I drank a flask of Ensure, and I gulped down some punch flavored Vitamin Water. The nap helped and the sun coming up helped a bit more. With the dawn, I felt better and began riding better.

Shadow now switched back to leapfrog support and, at one point, pulled over to a wide spot in the road. A RAAM official stopped to talk with them. It turned out to be Ross Muecke who I had known since 2007. He and I qualified for RAAM at the same time at the 2007 Tejas 500. Ross had also raced solo RAAM in 2010 but had DNFed in Ohio.

I was well up the road by the time Conice finished talking with Ross. The Shadow crew kept looking but could not find me as they chased me down. Michael thought maybe I had pulled over somewhere and they had passed me up. *Great, now we've lost our racer!* But they kept going and eventually saw a familiar speck up ahead on the road and they resumed their leapfrog role.

The sun climbed higher and my bowels began to move—I needed to take a dump. Bessie, with her closet bathroom, was up the road and not available and no way did I want to use the portable potty carried in Shadow. I asked Conice how far it was to the next town. He told me there were several small towns on the map but he doubted there would be anything open on a Sunday morning.

Sure enough, we went through Weston—and no restroom. I rode on through Segundo—again, no restroom. I was getting desperate. Conice had finally gotten phone service and talked with Joni in Bessie. They were only a few miles ahead so Bessie rendezvoused with me in Valdez. Finally, I was able to use the restroom.

While stopped, Joni decided to go ahead and make a shift change there at Valdez. Dan and crew took over leapfrog as I headed to Trinidad.

Team Dex arrived TS20. Trinidad, CO. 1130 miles. 115 RAAM hours.

Team Dex departed Trinidad, leaving the high Rockies behind on the receding western horizon. I would now be in the high plains with rolling hills as I headed to Kim, Colorado, the next time station. I had a good tailwind and there was little traffic, but limited pulloff areas, on the two-lane road. Damaris, driving Shadow, had to look for gates to local ranches to find a wide enough spot to move off of the road.

Dan made the most of the boredom of being in leapfrog mode. One time, as I approached Shadow, I looked ahead and saw Dan standing on the side of the road wearing his Crocodile Dundee hat. He was waving his arms like crazy. As I got closer I could see he was lifting the bottom of his tee shirt up over his chest. Dan had put on a sports bra and was flashing me. As I passed he said, "Hey big boy, you like this?"

It was hilarious. I don't think I ever laughed so hard on a bike. Damaris and Elaine were screaming "Waaahoooo!!".

I passed Dan and called out, "Hey, those are bigger than Joni's!"

Another time, I saw Dan ahead and he was lying on his belly, spread-eagled, right on the center of the yellow stripes of the highway. He had his camera pointed at me like a sniper in position. I was on my aerobars and I aimed my bike directly at him. I picked up as much speed as I could possibly muster at that point in the race. Dan held his position as I diverted at the very last moment to keep from running over him. As I whizzed by, he yelled, "Got it!"

Just a couple minutes later, I heard honking and yelling and carrying on. Here came Bessie and crew, and this time they had a surprise for me. The crew had taken orange duct tape and outlined the two windows above the cab of the RV to make it look like Bessie was wearing huge Team Dex orange glasses just like mine.

Everyone thought I bought the orange glasses just to have them for RAAM, but that was not true. I have always had problems with my glasses fogging up in cold, wet weather. Also, I have a severe astigmatism and without my prescription glasses I not only can't see very well, but I also get nauseous and have vertigo issues. So when my glasses fog up, I have two bad choices: either I keep them on and can't see, or I take them off, in which case I can't see and also get sick.

My glasses fogged up in the Texas Hill Country 600 RAAM qualifying race in March of 2011, but my super-duper crew chief had come up with a solution. She had decided since Rain-X was good on windshields, then it must be good on eyeglasses. Wrong! Rain-X is fine on glass. But Rain-X is not good on plastic lenses. My $300 prescription lenses crystallized and they soon looked like Spider Man's web. They were ruined.

So, I went online and shopped Warby Parker frames. They sent me several frames to try on and it just so happened that the frames that fitted my face best were orange. I could have ordered a different color but when I showed them to Joni, she replied, "They look artsy to me. I like them. Besides, you always wear bright colored socks. They'll go with your socks!"

I had no idea or intention that the glasses would become so popular in RAAM. But for whatever reason, the orange glasses became my trademark. I think it all started at the Evening With Dex fund raising dinner. The event was winding down and one of the guests raised his wine glass for a toast and said, "Here's to Team Dex!" Another guest raised his wine glass and said, "Here's to unfinished business!" And then Tony Hernandez raised his wine glass and said, "Here's to orange glasses!"

The orange glasses took off from there. They became a topic of conversation wherever I went. When RAAM started, people all across the nation and the world jumped on the orange glasses band wagon. Fans were following me online and they would buy some cheap, plastic orange frames from Wally World and wear the glasses at work and around town. Mothers were sending photos of their kids wearing orange glasses. My boss, Mike Wrob and four co-workers at Marathon Heater sent a photo of each of them holding up big letters that spelled out D E X A N—and, of course, they were all wearing orange glasses.

Soon after Bessie got her vision update with orange duct tape, Michael posted a photo on my Team Dex fan Facebook page that showed old, tired Bessie with her orange glasses parked next to a sleek, modern, decked-out, Class A, $1 million RAAM support RV. The post drew several witty comments:

> "That's right, you big fancy, shmancy, pompous, smirky, awesome, beautiful, RV."

> "We got spirit yes we do! We got Dex how about you!?"

> "The Dex shades win hands down!"

"Classic. Just like Dex. No glamour, just hard work and focus."

"Never judge a book by its cover, right Dex!"

Out on the Great Plains now, the temperature had risen as I neared Kim, Colorado. I looked ahead and saw Damaris standing on the side of the road with the purple flag, which meant, "Food, Gas, Lodging at next exit." Elaine yelled at me that she would have my favorite food for me at the next pull over. I rode with anticipation. I couldn't imagine what she was going to have for me since she couldn't cook like she did when she was in Bessie's full kitchen, but I was salivating nonetheless.

Within a couple of miles I saw Damaris waving the red flag. Yum, yum—time for Elaine's surprise!

I stopped and Dan immediately grabbed my bike so I didn't have to worry about where to lean it.

Elaine greeted me with, "Here you go Princess!"

She then proceeded to pop my bubble as she handed me one of those cardboard packages with a little tin can of chicken salad and one of those teeny, baby-sized spoons—the accompanying foil-wrapped crackers she opened up for me. So much for home cooking—at least she handed me a Dr. Pepper.

Five minutes for food and I was off again. As I pulled away, Elaine yelled, "Go Hidalgo!"

Hidalgo was the nickname Elaine's husband Kurt had given me. He said I reminded him of the movie about the horse named Hidalgo in the Ocean of Fire horse race. Just like RAAM, it was over a 3000-mile distance, but this race was held in the Arabian Desert and was restricted to the finest Arabian horses ever bred; only the purest and noblest lines, owned by the greatest royal families, were invited to the race. However, a wealthy sheik invited an American, Frank T. Hopkins, and his small mustang horse, Hidalgo, to enter the race for the first time, where Hopkins and Hidalgo were pushed to extremes they had never experienced. For Hopkins, the race became not only a matter of pride and honor, but a race for his very survival as he and his horse attempted the impossible. The same was holding true for me and RAAM.

What Kurt may not have realized is that I had something else in common with the movie other than just being the little wild mustang among thoroughbreds. In real life Hopkins was named Far Rider by a Lakota Indian Chief, but not because of his horse Hidalgo or his long races. The Chief called him Far Rider because he was far from himself, or lost from "home." Lance Armstrong has described ultra cycling racers as being lost, as if they were looking for something they could never find. Maybe Kurt and Lance knew more about me than I realized. *I wonder what I am missing. I wonder what I search for everyday on my bike.*

Team Dex arrived TS21. Kim, CO. 1200 miles.
121 RAAM hours.

Greg Cheyne: "That is some of the most beautiful country in the world... Next to the Colorado Rockies!"

Roy: "Out-freaking-standing Dex! You'll continue to be in our prayers, and you can best be believing that when the City of Del Rio celebrates your accomplishment, we are going to be there. Damn Dex, when I grow up I wanna be just like you."

Dolly: "Dex and Team Dex, you guys are truly amazing. We are in complete awe of all of you. It takes moxie to do what you are doing and we are so proud of you. God Bless you, we love you all so much and anxiously await your return."

Danny: "Dex, it is a treat to follow you from Oceanside. You have touched people you know and people you don't know. You have given people hope. Your drive is unshakable. Be proud also for following a dream and going after it."

Chapter 8

MY HALLUCINATORY FRIENDS

It takes "stuff" to be able to do RAAM. The kind of stuff that works. Real stuff. Stuff that you can feel from deep inside. The inherent stuff that comes from childhood values and how you were raised as a kid. The kind of stuff you get from your favorite high school teacher. Stuff that comes from your heart, not your legs. Stuff that you can't go down to Walmart and buy.

The "stuff" of RAAM is about heart, inner strength and discovering the magic deep in our souls. We all have deep reserves, but most do not realize it. RAAM is about having the passion and the courage to tap in to those reserves that we *all* have.

I know many guys who can bury me in the shorter 100-mile, 12-hour or 24-hour races. They have the speed and talent that it takes to hammer out those fast miles. Oh, what I would give to have their legs and their youth. But what some of them don't have is the heart to push forward when their legs scream, "I quit!" When a racer gets to the point where every muscle aches, every pedal stroke is a struggle, and nausea rules their gastro-intestinal tract, they can think of 1000 reasons not to continue. The negative thoughts begin to creep in. *This wind is eating my lunch. Why is there always one more hill? I've already done a great job, no one could blame me for dropping out now. What if I permanently injure myself? Why don't I just drop out now and save myself for my next race? I need to sleep. I really need to sleep. Oh, how good a pillow would feel. If I stop now, I could sleep for days.*

Sure, they can think of all kinds of reasons to quit, but what matters is if they can think of at least one reason to keep going. At this lowest of low points, can they come up with this thought, for example: *Quitting is not an option!* There comes a time for every rider when RAAM is no longer about racing—it becomes about not quitting.

Team Dex departed the Kim, Colorado time station in the mid-afternoon and, hooray, no more leapfrog! Even though it was daylight, direct follow was now legal from here all the way to the finish line. The route from Kim to Walsh, Colorado was mixed, with many low rollers and flat grasslands in this long traverse of the high plains. Normally, this might be called relatively "easy" terrain for a cyclist, but nothing is ever easy in RAAM. The afternoon temperatures climbed as we left the Rocky Mountains behind until the temperature gauge in Shadow's dashboard read 99 degrees. And, just to make it a bit more challenging, we immediately encountered 25 to 35 mph cross winds; I was actually leaning into the wind just to keep my bicycle upright. Then, when the gusts would dwindle for an instant, I would nearly tip over the opposite direction.

All of this did not help my forearms, which were already bruised and tender from the long hours of riding on my aerobars. Since I would be spending even more hours in that position now that we were on the Colorado plains (and very soon, the flatlands of Kansas) Joni improvised some thick elbow pads to help soften the pressure.

Three tall grain elevators marked my arrival in the small community of Pritchett, Colorado and we found the streets nearly deserted in this one-horse town on this lazy, hot Sunday afternoon. I stopped at the one traffic signal in the entire town near an older lady who was standing on the sidewalk in front of the local bakery. She stared in bewilderment at this idiot on a bicycle being followed by a van covered with decals and speakers blaring out the U2 hit, *I Still Haven't Found What I'm Looking For*. She was close enough I was scared she could smell me. I tried to wipe some of the road grime off my lips and stubbly grey facial growth. *Maybe I won't smell so bad if I wipe some of this stuff off.* Even though she never asked the question, I knew she had to be wondering what in the world was going on. I stood there wearing a crazy looking helmet with microphone sticking out one side and rear-view mirror sticking out the other side. I looked at her and said, "I'm in a bicycle race."

Looking totally puzzled and even less impressed, she yelled back, "What race?"

As the light changed, I stood on my pedals, turned my head in her direction and proudly proclaimed, "I'm racing across America!"

Dex Tooke

Team Dex arrived TS22. Walsh, CO. 1269 miles. 126 RAAM hours.

Conice's crew manned Shadow as we departed Walsh and 14 miles later I heard Anika's soft-spoken voice announce over the PA system, "Colorado, DONE! We are now in Kansas!" Please excuse me Kansas, but I have to admit the first 100 miles or so in your state was my least favorite. The roads were totally flat and the scenery boring. I mean, c'mon! Once you've seen one acre of corn, you've seen it all. It was just miles and miles of very flat, straight, two lane roads with narrow shoulders, and I must admit I don't do flats well. I am the type of rider that needs to switch things up. I need inclines that let me stand every now and then. I need hills that permit me to grab a couple of gears every so often. I just cannot get into a groove and ride the same gear in the same position for mile after mile.

On we went across the flats, as the sun slowly dropped to the west and darkness approached. Any rider that does much night riding will quickly tell you that things aren't quite the same on a bike once the sun goes down. You totally lose your depth perception and you have no idea how far up the road or off to the side of the road you are actually seeing. Trees and bushes play tricks on your eyes. You begin to see shapes and forms that make you wonder what you are actually seeing. Sometimes you even think some of those weird shapes may be reaching out to grab you. You sometimes dodge things that really aren't there to begin with. Now, all of these things I mention happen on *any* night ride, but just imagine if you have already ridden over 1200 miles and you are totally exhausted and mentally incapacitated. It can be extremely stressful.

It was "dark thirty," I figured. I had no idea what time it really was because I couldn't see my bike computer. I was pedaling down a very flat, boring two-lane road. It was pitch black with no moon. There hadn't been anything but corn fields on both sides for what seemed like 30 or 40 miles. Conice was playing *Green Grass and High Tides* by the Outlaws and I asked him to crank it up. I looked over to my right and saw a white light in the cornfield beside the road. It was too dark for me to make anything out, but I figured it was some farmer plowing his fields in one of those state-of-the-art tractors, one of those machines that have air conditioning and a stereo. *Heck,* I thought, *he probably has an ice chest and cold beer in there. Maybe he's even watching the Royals play the Yankees. I wonder if he has a remote control?*

The light atop the tractor was moving at just about the same speed as I was. Being bored, I decided to grab a couple of gears, stand on my pedals and do a short interval to see if I could pull up beside him and check things out. I sprinted hard for nearly a minute and I didn't gain any ground on the light.

Then, I heard Conice's voice over my headset asking, "What the heck are you doing?"

I disregarded the question.

A couple of minutes later I went through another similar interval, this time even more determined to pull up beside the white light. But again, I was unsuccessful. This time Michael came on the radio and demanded, "What the hell are you trying to do? This is no time to be doing intervals!"

I paid just as much attention to Michael as I had to Conice.

After I caught my breath, I grabbed a couple of gears once more and pushed it for a third time. I was bound and determined to catch that farmer and his Nascar tractor. By this time, my paranoia was assuring me the farmer was watching me—every time I would get a little close, he would gun his John Deere. I gave it everything I had and still I couldn't catch the imagined green machine.

After my little interval session I was zonked. My hamstrings were cramping and the lactic acid had built up in my legs. I couldn't keep doing this. I finally held out an imaginary white flag of surrender to Mr. Oliver Wendell Douglas—you win Mr. Green Acres!

I continued to ride for another three or four miles with the white light staying directly in front and to the right of me. Then it hit me and I felt like a total fool. I looked ahead and saw the white light once more, this time in its true form. The white light I had been chasing and that I had thought was a farmer on his plow machine was actually my exhaustion and sleep deprivation playing tricks with my depth perception. Instead of chasing something that I thought was about 10 feet tall and within 20 yards of the side of the road, I had been chasing a 60-foot tall grain elevator that sat a good ¼ mile off the road. Kansas wins!

Team Dex arrived TS23. Ulysses, KS. 1323 miles. 131 hours.

I guess all the climbing in Arizona and Colorado had finally taken its toll on my knees. I was starting to get pain on the lateral aspect of my left knee, so Conice decided it would be best if he went ahead and stabilized both knees with Rock Tape. He also gave me 800mg of Ibuprofen.

After gobbling down bean burritos, pasta salad, two Eskimo Pies and a Dr. Pepper, I was back on the beautiful, dark roads of Kansas with Dan and crew following in Shadow. Dan began a constant chatter into my headset, telling me about his bike racing days when he was going to school in Argentina. Man, I wished I could race like that guy. I just listened in envy.

Grain elevators and corn fields continued to be my only source of scenery. Every now and then I would hear the humming sound of a water well pumping water out of a canal to the thirsty fields. I was so sleepy that I was beginning to weave on the road. My head kept nodding and it was difficult for me to distinguish when I was awake and when I was nodding off.

Sleep deprivation was taking control. Occasionally I would see the flicker of Shadow's headlight beams in my helmet mirror. The flicker was starting to play tricks on me. I started hallucinating that the flickers were friends of mine riding along with me. I called them my "hallucinatory friends." My imaginary friends were very real to me, though. They were riding right there with me in the dark night on these lonely, flat, straight, endless Kansas miles. They kept me company. I could see them and talk to them. I could confide in them and tell them my inner most thoughts and feelings. I knew they were loyal and would never share my secrets.

Dan was observing my behavior and knew I would have to go down soon for a sleep. He spoke to me over the headset, "Dex, you are starting to weave. I think you should start looking for a wide spot in the road and we will put you down for a short power nap before daybreak. Then maybe sunrise will perk you up."

I replied, but I wasn't replying to Dan. I thought it was one of my friends talking to me and so I replied back, "I remember the time we were both in Cozumel on a night dive. There were all these Moray eels sticking their heads out of the coral. Their mouths were wide open and their teeth showing. Do you remember that?"

Dan didn't answer me. He just turned to Elaine and said, "Oh, boy!"

The SOP, or standard operating procedure, when I stop for any reason, whether it be to eat, use the restroom or go down for a sleep, is for the navigator to immediately exit Shadow and come up to me as quickly as possible to hold my bike. This way I don't have to worry about finding a place to lean my bike. The navigator just stands there and holds it for me while the domestique helps me with whatever I need to do.

On this dark night in Kansas, as I was riding with my trusty "friends", I finally saw a turnout on the left side of the road. It was nothing more than a paved culvert next to a canal. I motioned with my left arm that I was going to pull over and Shadow's lights followed me to the wide spot.

I got off my bike and the first thing I did was hand my bike to my friend. The only problem was that my friend was hallucinatory and my bike fell directly onto the pavement. Dan saw what was going on and was running toward me yelling, "Dex, don't do it! Don't!" But it was too late. I had just thrown my bike down on the road, right on the drive train side. Dan quickly picked the bike up and made sure I hadn't damaged it in any way.

Elaine helped me remove my helmet and my shoes. I crawled like a wounded soldier on top of the thin foam bed in the back of Shadow and I was asleep before my head hit, friends and all.

Thirty minutes, later Elaine was waking me up and telling me to drink my Perpetuem. I did so reluctantly, calling her names under my breath all the while.

Team Dex arrived TS24. Montezuma, KS. 1374 miles. 136 RAAM hours.

Joe's crew rotated onto duty. That meant that Em and Joe would be fighting over the headset while Joni would probably be catching catnaps as domestique.

I was in a foul mood. What was new? Days of sleep deprivation affect different people in different ways. In my case, I think it mostly manifests itself in the form of irritability and paranoia. I tend to get very grumpy and think everyone is plotting against me. The crew can do nothing right when I get this grumpy. If Joni offers me Vitamin Water, I get mad and say I want Dr. Pepper. If Em brings out my Texas Hill Country jersey for me to wear, then I tell her I want my DR FART jersey. If Joe puts water in my hydration system, he doesn't put in enough ice. When I am in this paranoid state I think my crew is keeping secrets from me. I get suspicious when I see them covering their lips and whispering when I am around. They suddenly stop talking when I am around and I think, *I wonder what they are saying. I wonder what they are plotting. I bet they are going to sabotage the wheels on my bike so they can go home early. I know it. I just know it.*

I ached all over. My elbows hurt, my saddle sores hurt, my knees hurt. I don't normally like to play the age card, but I was feeling very old about then. My mind was wandering and I was starting to hallucinate again. When I get into this mental state, it is extremely difficult for me to distinguish time. It is like I am in some kind of time travel machine and I can't figure out what is real time or what is fantasy time.

I remembered commuting to work one day in Del Rio on my trusty 20+ year old Trek 1400. I keep it equipped with panniers to carry all my stuff. It was early morning and the sun wasn't even up yet. I stopped at a convenience store to use the restroom and as I walked in, I noticed two Bud Light delivery guys setting up a beer display. They began whispering and talking the instant I entered. I had my suspicions they were trying to keep me from hearing what they were saying, but it didn't bother me, I just kept walking toward the restroom. I assumed they recognized me and may have even heard the radio program I had done the day before—Travis Mariner, aka Mr. T the sports genius of KDLK Radio, had invited me on his live sports radio program for an interview.

When I exited the bathroom, the two beer guys started whispering again. As I walked by, I overheard one of them say, "I didn't think he was that old!"

Now, out here in the middle of the Kansas flatlands, I felt every bit as old as the two beer guys thought I was.

The flat miles in Kansas were boring. Finally, I spoke into my helmet microphone and asked Joe how much further it was to Greenburg. I couldn't believe it when he told me another 44 miles—and I was still encountering strong right to left crosswinds. RAAM officials issued a safety warning to the crew in Shadow to be sure and maintain a visual with their rider at all times as visibility can become very limited during Kansas dust storms. Great, just what I needed. Luckily, the dust stayed away and I didn't have visibility difficulties.

Team Dex arrived TS25. Greensburg, KS. 1440 miles. 142 RAAM hours.

Joe's crew was still in Shadow and they pulled in behind me as I headed out of Greensburg toward Pratt. I felt like I would puke if I saw one more grain elevator—I hated those things. I picked up a good tailwind but I was so sleepy I couldn't keep my bike on the road; I was swerving all across the lane. Even though it had only been eight hours since my last sleep, Joni decided to put me down again.

I crawled into my little cubby hole in Shadow and Joni let me sleep for 30 wonderful minutes. I awoke very slowly and wasn't talkative, ignoring anything Joni or any of the crew said to me. It was as if I were a little first-grader throwing a temper tantrum. I just got on my bike and started riding.

Em got on the headset and started talking to me even though I wasn't talking back to her. She told me that Michele Santilhano had sent me a Facebook message. Michele was a solo racer in 2010—one of my favorite competitors—and we had formed a strong RAAM camaraderie. She finished just 1.5 hours before the cut-off that year. I so admired her. I had cried with joy and pride when I saw her walk up to the podium at the 2010 awards banquet. Em read me the message from Michele: "You have this Dex. Defeat your demons. Don't let them win!"

Team Dex arrived TS26 Pratt, KS. 1471 miles. 145 RAAM hours.

About 20 miles outside of Pratt I saw Bessie up ahead parked on the side of the road. Bessie's crew was standing on the side of the road and Conice's crew was in follow mode behind me in Shadow. Both Joe and Dan had their cameras out and snapped away as I approached. Everyone was yelling and cheering, but I was a zombie and had no idea what was going on. Then Conice got on the headset and told me, "Welcome to the halfway point Dex. You have 1494.7 miles to go!"

I looked at the roadway and the crew had painted "Go, Dex, Go", "Halfway there", and "Piece of Cake" on the pavement in bright-colored chalk. This was all cool and fun except for one thing: it totally depressed me. I had been and was still feeling like crap for the last several hours. All kinds of negative thoughts flew into my head. *This is halfway? I'll never make it! Still 1500 miles to go? Are they sure? This has to be a mistake!*

Joe snapped photos of me as I passed and he captured the look in my eyes. He would later say that when he saw me at that point, he didn't think I would make it to Annapolis.

Thankfully, I got a little bit of a pick-me-up shortly after that. Conice let me know via the headset that a rider was approaching us from behind. It was Steven Perezluha, the youngest solo RAAM competitor, who had turned 20 just before the start of the race. Even at his young age, he had a lot of ultra racing and cross country experience. This was by no means his first attempt at a multi-day event. He came from good ultra blood, too—his uncle and crew member is Danny Chew. Danny, an eight-time RAAM veteran, was also RAAM champion in 1996 and 1998. Danny is known as the Million Mile Man because he is on pace to log one million career lifetime miles on his bike. So, Danny's young nephew, Steven, pulled up beside me looking very fresh and very fast. He maneuvered his bike close to mine and wrapped his right arm around my shoulder. He leaned in close and said, "You know when to quit don't you?"

I was puzzled. *Quit? What is this guy talking about?* I asked, a bit perplexed, "What did you say?"

He repeated his question, this time with an answer, "You know when to quit don't you? AT THE FINISH LINE! Keep it up buddy! You inspire me!"

I thought it was pretty cool that the young met the old like this on the road in the toughest bicycle race in the world!

A few miles further along I saw a guy walking down the shoulder of the highway. He walked right out in front of me and I had to stop. Conice got on the headset and asked, "Why are you stopping? Do you need something?"

I said, "That guy walked right out in front me!"

Conice replied, "Dex, there is no one there. Just keep going."

Michael said, "Yep, he's hallucinating again!"

Team Dex arrived TS27. Maize, KS. 1548 miles. 150 RAAM hours.

About 10 miles before we arrived at TS27, Conice had received a call from the War Room in Tucson advising us of a detour about four miles beyond Maize. A storm had come through and had blown a power line down across the road and utility crews had the road blocked.

I stopped at the Kwik Shop at the TS but I didn't even dismount my bike. Joni had decided we would change crews at the TS without really stopping. Dan's crew had their ice chest and gear bags ready for a flying crew change.

Then, a few minutes later, I experienced yet another pleasant meeting on the road. About two miles past the time station, a car pulled up beside me on my left. His passenger window was down and the driver yelled, "Dex!" I looked over and it was Bart Boma. Bart, was a DR FART then stationed at Laughlin Air Force Base in Del Rio and, as a bike racer himself, he had been instrumental in helping me prepare for RAAM. He and his family were returning from their vacation in Wisconsin and had been keeping track of Team Dex progress. Bart also had another friend in RAAM on an eight-person team he was tracking.

I was totally shocked and excited to see Bart; he really lifted my spirits. Bart was also a long time friend of Dan's, so Bart got to see Dan, too. We all spoke just for a short time as Bart didn't want to cause me to get a time penalty by talking to me while we were moving. It was really great seeing him.

Shortly after that we came to the detour. A RAAM official advised us the detour would be routing us onto the interstate and I would be allowed to put my bike in Shadow and ride in the van for the short distance until we exited the interstate. I got a whole 10-minute nap during the process. Bessie stayed on the interstate and took the fast route to El Dorado, Kansas while I pedaled the back roads. It was now dark and I could see that the storm that caused the detour was severe, but it was well ahead of me and moving east. I watched the lightening in the dark skies directly in front of me all the way to El Dorado.

Team Dex arrived TS28. El Dorado, KS. 1583 miles. 154 RAAM hours.

Bessie was waiting in the parking lot of the Walmart Supercenter at TS28. I wasn't scheduled to go down for a sleep but I wanted to go down. My will was dwindling; I just didn't have the drive. I wasn't any more tired or exhausted or sleep deprived than most other times during RAAM, but I was mentally weak. Joni gave in and allowed me to go down for a short nap in Bessie. What a treat! I not only got to sleep on a real mattress, but she also let me remove my grungy cycling jersey and shorts. It felt so good to feel that sheet against my skin as I lay on that memory foam queen size bed.

Joni let me sleep for 90 minutes—an hour longer than we had planned—and she medicated my saddle sores. I even got to take a dump on a real toilet in Bessie. She helped me put on a fresh cycling jersey and shorts. Elaine fed me fresh scrambled eggs with toast and honey. I love milk and I even got to drink a cold glass of it! Of course, all of this took precious time and this was exactly the reason Joni had been keeping Bessie off-limits to me.

Dan and crew were still on duty in Shadow and the first thing I did when I got back on the bike was ask Dan how long I had taken at El Dorado. He said my off bike time was a little over two hours. I nearly died. My paranoia engulfed me. I just knew I had just blown my RAAM. First of all, I took an unscheduled sleep break. Second, I had been a softie and slept in the luxury of Bessie. And third, I had taken my time by eating high on the hog.

I started rambling on to Dan via the headset. I said, "My RAAM is over. I have let everyone down. A real RAAM racer wouldn't take a rest like that. I don't deserve to finish RAAM. I don't deserve to be a part of RAAM. I didn't have to sleep, but I did. Everyone in Del Rio will be disappointed in me. There is no way I can ever make up the lost ground."

Dan kept trying to reassure me that it wasn't that bad and that my RAAM wasn't over. I got very ugly with Dan. I started calling him a liar. I accused him of telling me lies just to make things sound better than they really were. Dan again tried to convince me that it really wasn't that bad, but I would not listen to him—my paranoia was too strong. I accused him of patronizing me and I had told every one of my crew months before

RAAM had begun that I would not tolerate being patronized. I told them, "Don't you dare ever tell me how good I look when I know I look like crap. Don't you dare tell me how great I am and how fast I am going when I know good and well I am not." And now here was my best friend, Dan, telling me that everything was going to be okay.

"Dan," I said, "don't you dare patronize me. You are lying to me. And I know it!"

Dan started reading the numbers to me to prove I was still on track to finish RAAM within the cut-off time, but I wouldn't listen. I finally told him, "I'm not talking to you anymore. Don't talk to me!"

I guess Dan figured, *fine*, because I didn't hear another word from him and I didn't say another word to him for the rest of his shift. I look back on it now and I don't know how in the world I could ever treat a dear friend such as Dan with so much disrespect.

Team Dex arrived TS29. Yates Center, KS. 1647 miles. 162 hours.

It was about 8:00 a.m. local time when I left Yates Center and Joe and crew were back on duty in the follow vehicle. The sun was now up and I was awake enough that I could at least ride down the road without weaving. I was thankful we were out of the flatlands of Kansas. Now the route was constant rollers and I was in much better spirits.

About three miles out from the time station, Donncha Cuttriss from Ireland pulled up beside me. We were on a four-lane divided highway with wide shoulders so I was able to ride with Donncha and visit for a little bit, which I thoroughly enjoyed. We both knew the physical and mental condition we were in and we both quietly shared what we had endured and would continue to endure. We both knew the score. Donncha's thick Irish accent was actually easier to understand than had been Joshua Kench's New Zealand accent. I jokingly told Donncha my crew had a six-pack of Coors Light in the van and asked him if he wanted a cold one. He replied in his Irish brogue, "I only drink stout ale!"

About 9:00 a.m. Texas time, Rudy, the DJ from KDLK Radio in Del Rio, phoned Shadow. The radio station did live phone interviews every morning and again in the afternoon on Mr. T's sports programs. They would interview whichever domestique or navigator happened to be on duty in Shadow at the time and Dexans in Del Rio tuned in for the live interviews.

After the interview, I asked Joe to call the Bank and Trust and give them an update. Joe called and spoke with Maricela Saenz, telling her that I was in Kansas and everything was on schedule. Joe told me after the call that they were happy he'd called and that the only thing everyone at the bank wanted to know was what kind of music I listened to while I was racing.

Joe then called Bob Hilton, a close friend of mine who lived in Pennsylvania and who I knew was following me on the internet. Bob was thrilled that Joe had called. He told Joe he was finding it hard to work since he constantly found himself sitting in front of his computer checking the Team Dex progress. He had six bookmarks on his computer: my ultradex site, my Facebook page, the RAAM website, my GPS tracker, Google earth for the route, and the weather channel to see what kind of weather I was in. He said he just constantly went from site to site checking for updates. Bob also said he actually sent an email to ABC sports telling them they were missing the boat by not covering RAAM or at least providing updates. Thirty years ago, ABC Sport's had covered the entire 3000 miles of the original race with commentators Jim Lampley and ultra athlete Diana Nyad on the *Wide World of Sports*.

Team Dex arrived TS30. Fort Scott, KS. 1706 miles. 166 RAAM hours.

Julie: "Go, DEX! Watching you every day!"

Malcolm R: "UN-BELIEVABLE. He is truly an inspiration to everyone and anyone who rides. Go Dex Go."

John Ehrke: "Looking good Dex! Your friends in Big Bend are thinking of you and sending wishes of good will to you and Team Dex."

Eddy and Sherry: "We pray that the weather will be perfect for you. May the LORD watch over all of you!"

Anthony Kusenberger: "Great weather, great guy, great team. Keep it up. Great job."

Chapter 9

OOOH, MISSOURI

Damaris and Elaine had fed me a fried egg sandwich with lots of extra sharp cheddar cheese at the Ft. Scott time station. The sandwich hit the spot, but my instinct told me it wouldn't be long before I would have to take a dump and I couldn't afford to just sit around waiting for the urge. Conice's crew was scheduled in Shadow, but I asked Joni to take over as navigator instead of Conice; I wanted her close so she could treat my saddle sores after the intestinal urge hit. I also thought it would be good for Joni to get a chance to crew with Anika and Michael since she and Anika have so much in common, both being art teachers. And, of course, Michael and Joni had worked many hours together on vehicle preparation in the months preceding RAAM.

Team Dex entered Missouri about five miles past Ft. Scott, Kansas and Michael got on the PA system with the announcement, "Kansas, DONE!"

The roads of Missouri were not smooth, to say the least. They had more abrupt curves and, if there were shoulders at all, they were very narrow. The climbs through the Ozarks were shorter but much steeper than the climbs in the Rockies, and the traffic was a lot faster and in much closer quarters than was the case in the wide open space of the West.

As I was nearing Nevada, Missouri I noticed a RAAM rider up ahead who turned out to be Randy Mouri from Fairfax, Virginia. As I approached, I noticed he was wearing a mechanical device for a problem known as Shermer's neck.

Shermer's neck is an unusual but common injury among RAAM competitors and it got its name from Michael Shermer who was one of the original four racers in the inaugural *Great American Bicycle Race*—the race that started this entire crazy nonsense of racing across America on a bicycle some 30 years ago. Michael developed the neck problem in his

1983 race as he was going through Illinois. Over just a short period of time, his neck muscles became extremely weak and sore, and shortly after that he lost complete control of them.

Shermer's neck can be as much psychologically demoralizing as it is physically debilitating. A grown man—or woman—suddenly regresses to the infant stage and can't even hold the head in an upright position, which makes it nearly impossible to see the road ahead. In the past, racers and crew have come up with some bizarre mechanical devices to give support to the neck and head. In 2009, Paul Danhaus, suffering from Shermer's, duct taped a Pringle's Potato Chip can vertically to his handlebars. He then taped female Maxi Pads to the top of the can for padding. He rode for two more days to finish RAAM with his chin resting on the Maxi Pads. Other riders have utilized bungee cords attached to their helmet on one end and to their saddles on the other just to hold their heads up so they could see the road and thus ride safely. In Randy's case, he was wearing a C-collar used by paramedics in emergency trauma situations to stabilize patients with possible cervical injuries.

I pulled up alongside him for a short chat. "Hey Randy, how is it going?" I asked.

Without turning his head toward me, he replied, "Goin' good. How about yourself?"

"I'm hanging in there. How long have you had Shermer's?"

"I started developing it in Kansas. Right now it isn't too bad. I have the C-collar on more for prevention than anything else."

I told him, "Kansas is way too early to get Shermer's. You must be in misery."

He explained, "The pain isn't bad. Wearing the collar, it's actually more comfortable for me to stand to pedal than it is to sit."

I said, "Geez. I tip my hat to you!"

We parted company soon after that and I didn't see Randy again until Annapolis.

Well, you know what they say, "When you gotta go, you gotta go." Not long after my conversation with Randy, and a bit closer to Nevada, Missouri, the urge finally hit. I alerted Joni and we found a wide spot in the road for Shadow. The wind was blowing hard and it was difficult for Michael, Anika and Joni to hold up the privacy tarp as I sat totally humiliated on my aluminum throne. Behind the tarp, I could hear the nearby traffic zooming down the highway. Actually, though, I was so out of it that I really didn't care who saw me at that point. *Peek all you want Missouri! I could care less!*

After Joni medicated my butt, I was back on the road, but I was weaving terribly. The shoulder was narrow and the traffic heavy. I could not keep awake and my head kept bouncing around like a bobblehead doll, so Joni made a safety decision that I should go down for yet another unscheduled sleep. Michael spotted a small, barely paved country road up ahead and Joni got on the PA and told me to take it. I rode about quarter of a mile down the country road where we parked halfway off the road. There was a nearby farm house with a big, grassy yard and a huge shade tree. Michael walked up to the farm house and knocked. A lady came to the door and Michael asked permission for us to park under her tree while I went down for a short sleep. The lady was very nice and even invited us inside to sleep if it was necessary. Michael thanked her kindly for the offer but explained it wasn't necessary and we would be just fine in the yard.

Michael and Anika stayed outside under the tree while I slept. Joni stayed in the van and called the War Room to let them know we were taking a sleep break just off of the race route. I slept for 60 minutes and then was back on the road. When the crew in Bessie heard I was going down for a sleep, they pulled in to a Kwiky Shop in El Dorado Springs, just ahead of us. When I came by Bessie, Conice relieved Joni as navigator and rejoined his crew.

I don't know how, but I continued to push. I don't know what it is inside of me that keeps me going at such times, but there is something. It must be that same something that drives me to turn a 14-mile daily commute to work into 25 miles by riding extra distance. I live about seven miles outside of Del Rio, Texas near Lake Amistad and I work in town at Marathon Heater, a manufacturer of electrical heating elements. Pedro Guerra, a co-worker, would see me ride right past the turn-off to Marathon every morning—headed for my extra miles—as if I didn't see the turn. He would kid with me saying he was going to put a big electrical sign on the side of the road that read, "Dex, turn here!"

Also, in the months before RAAM, I would do specific sleep deprivation training rides—and at this point in RAAM maybe they were starting to pay off.

I remember one Friday afternoon I had commuted home on my bike. I was totally beat from work. My brain was fried and all I wanted to do was sit down in my chair and try to decompress. I ate a light supper about 7:00 pm. and by 8:00 p.m. I was ready for my ritual bowl of Cheerios before bed. As I reached into the cabinet to get my favorite cereal bowl, I thought to myself, *I am dead tired. I am beat. Now is the time I need to be training for RAAM. I don't need to train for RAAM when I am fresh and feel like riding 100 miles. The only time I'm going to be fresh in RAAM is the first day. I'll be exhausted from then on.* So, I put the cereal back in the pantry, mixed up some Perpetuem, Pedialyte and filled my water bottles, then I went out to my gym and put my lights on my bike.

It was 8:30 p.m. when I hit the road. I rode for 187 miles. It was just turning dawn when I came back to my house. I was too tired to even shower. I collapsed in my bed and awoke about two hours later. After taking a quick leak, I stumbled into the kitchen to get a drink of water. Joni was standing at the sink washing dishes. I turned to her and said, "Damn, I am dead tired!"

Without hesitation she replied, "You look like crap! Go get on your bike and ride."

I first looked at her in disbelief. Then I quickly realized she was right, so I put my gear back on and hit the road. I came back 80 miles later.

Team Dex arrived TS31. Weaubleau, MO. 1772 miles. 174 RAAM hours.

The traffic congestion lessened somewhat once the sun went down and the stars came out, but the steep rolling hills certainly didn't cease; it continued to be one climb after another. I decided I wanted to try to ride through the night until about 4:00 a.m. before going down for a short sleep so I could then get up at dawn to welcome the morning sun.

Jeric Wilhelmsen and his media crew met up with me during the night on one of the climbs and did a rolling interview. Of course, the instant they pulled up beside me I started going 3 mph faster—after all, I couldn't let them see me riding too slowly.

Jeric told me, "This is your year, Dex. You are doing great. How are you feeling? How is 2011 going compared to 2010?"

I lied to him, "I feel great. I'm taking it easy. I'm staying on the bike more than last year and I'm more efficient."

He ended the interview by asking me, "What is your expected arrival time at the finish line?"

"One minute before cut-off time!" I responded.

Too bad I couldn't have a media crew beside me the whole time—I would certainly ride a lot faster!

Dan was cranking out the Rocker songs on my sound system. *Ain't No Sunshine* by Bill Withers made for a good climbing song, then the 5 O'Clock Rocker's theme song, *Fat Bottom Girls* by Queen played. I stood on my pedals and danced. The sound system started catching noise interference shortly after that and microphone hog Dan couldn't resist the opportunity to take over the PA system to read a few Facebook comments to me.

One of the posts was from Michael T., my webmaster, who had put his statistical summary on my Team Dex fan page: "To all Dexans, a heartfelt thanks to you. This site has almost 5,000 active users and 2,356 posts have been made since Oceanside with 107,287 views of these posts from even more users. You ARE the most active fan base in RAAM. Also, Ultradex receives 300-425 visitors per day with awesome posts of support. THANK YOU & KEEP IT COMING. Also, welcome to our new followers from Iraq, Hong Kong, and New Zealand.

Then Dan read off some of the comments that followed Michael's post.

Allison Hilton Jones: "Following Team Dex is like being addicted to crack (I can only imagine)! If I don't get my regular fix, I start getting jittery and suffering from withdrawal. Following you, every pedal of the way from Pittsburgh, PA. Go, Team Dex!!!"

Linda Guerrette: "And who knew the impact Dex would have on other people's lives when he conjured up this wacky idea to race his bike across the country solo. Impactful, dude. You rock. Thanks for taking us along for this simply incredible ride."

Patty Ryedelius: "Just keep it going Dex & team. You have such an awesome spirit for the RAAM cause. You are a very inspirational soul."

Bill Cullins: "Keep it rolling, Dex. San Angelo is cheering you on!"

Then Dan read a post Joni wrote to all the fans letting them know how good of a job they were all doing: "The Team Dex crew is absolutely amazing. They are one of the many reasons Dex is able to do what he is doing. A world of gratitude to all who are supporting the love of my life. From Joni."

I continued climbing the Ozark rollers through the night. I had three tough climbs of 6% grade as I approached the Lake of the Ozarks, a beautiful place, even in the dark. As I crossed the bridge I could see the expensive yachts quietly docked in the harbor, their lights and outlines reflected on the still, black water.

Team Dex arrived TS32. Camdenton, MO. 1821 miles. 179 RAAM hours.

Bessie and crew were waiting for me at TS32. I was scheduled for a sleep break and they planned on getting some much needed rest, too. Camdenton was really a cool time station. Eric Johnston, a diehard RAAM fan and volunteer, was the lone station captain and he manned it 24/7. When we arrived he was very apologetic because a storm had just come through and blown down his make-shift canopy and table.

Eric remembered me from 2010. He and I also had a mutual friend in RAAM, official, Johnny Boswell. Eric had promised Johnny he would get his picture taken with me and send it ahead to Johnny. Eric also let us fill the water tank in Bessie with a water hose from the convenience store.

Even though it was close to 2:00 a.m. local time, the convenience store was a flurry of activity. There were two police squad cars out front and the officers were questioning some drunk in the parking lot.

I went to sleep in the van while most of the crew slept in Bessie. Dan pulled out a sleeping bag and slept on the pavement near Eric's table. Joni let me sleep for two entire hours.

Every time I awake from a sleep, I have no idea where I am or what I am doing. Joni has to remind me that I am in a bicycle race called RAAM. It usually takes me an hour, or at least until the sun comes up, before I figure out the score and know the "que pasa".

I was talking to Joe on the headset as I left Camdenton in my mental stupor and he asked me if I knew where I was and what I was doing. I replied, "I'm on my Trek and I'm riding to El Paso." Two strikes against me. My Trek back-up bike was riding in the rack on top of Shadow and no way was I headed west to El Paso. This young man was headed east even if he didn't realize it.

Even in the wee hours before dawn, the traffic was considerable as I again crossed the Lake of the Ozarks and Osage Beach. When the sun finally appeared, I saw a roadside billboard that advertised Hannibal, Missouri. The sign showed a young boy with a big smile on his face and read, "Are we there yet?" *I only wish!*

The traffic was heavy on US 54. I had just taken the Jefferson City off-ramp and I was stopped at the traffic light at Stadium Boulevard. Bessie hadn't arrived yet, but I could see other RAAM support vehicles at TS33 across the street. When the light turned green, I clipped into my pedals and started across the intersection onto a street with two-way traffic and no shoulder.

Then as Joe described it later, the most horrific moment in Team Dex's RAAM occurred. A full-sized blue Tahoe sped across the intersection. The raging driver of the Tahoe went directly at Em, who was driving Shadow, and forced her off the road, then Em, Joe and Joni watched in terror as the Tahoe went full throttle toward me. I had no idea he was there. Joe estimated the Tahoe was probably doing 40-45 mph by this time and he aimed his truck directly at me. I felt a hard thud on my left shoulder as if I had been cold cocked by a NFL defensive back. The vehicle was a blur as it just kept going after he hit me. I was so pissed off I just yelled, "What the &%$#!" I raised my good arm at him just hoping he would look in his rear view mirror and see my rage.

He had hit me with his right outside mirror just as I was turning right into the time station. If I hadn't been turning, he would have run directly over me. The crew in Shadow had witnessed the hit-and-run and it had obviously been an intentional assault.

Em screamed, "Oh my God! Oh my God! He's been hit!"

Watching from the domestique seat in the van, Joni cried out, "These sons of bitches don't care about anything. I hate Missouri!"

Joe told Em, "Let's just get to Dex!"

I did not go down. Luckily I was able to keep my bike up and I pulled into the time station with Shadow pulling up behind me. Em immediately got out and came to hold my bike while Joe came to see if I was okay. Joni was screaming and cussing as she ran up the roadway trying to see the Tahoe and get a plate number. She began questioning everyone around. She wanted to know if there were any other eye witnesses.

My shoulder was bruised and tight. I had limited range of motion but it wasn't the kind of injury that would keep me from riding my bike. I went over to Em who was holding my bike. I couldn't see her eyes for her shades, but I could see tears running down her cheeks. I reassured her that there was nothing she could have done. She was obviously emotionally distraught.

Then, Joe came over to me. Words were not immediately spoken; the two brothers just looked at each other in the eye. I finally spoke to Joe, "This is RAAM. Let's go." We touched fists and prepared to race on.

Joni didn't have any luck finding witnesses and she could see I was up, walking and ready to ride. She was still so mad she didn't even ask about my injury but wanted to call the police. I told her, "No. The police will just want to file a report and it will take too much time. The clock is running. We have to move."

Team Dex arrived TS33. Jefferson City, MO. 1878 miles. 186 RAAM hours.

Em was too upset to continue driving, so Joni took the wheel while Em moved to the domestique post. Joni just kept saying, "Let's get out of this city and this state—the sooner the better!"

Navigation was tricky leaving the time station—the traffic was extremely heavy and we were headed right through downtown Jefferson City on Capitol Ave., passing directly by the Missouri State Capitol building. We finally made it through the crowded downtown district and headed out of town but, even so, trucks and cars were constantly honking and yelling at us. Joni was becoming even more enraged. She stayed right on my ass, blocking for me like she was in a battle. Just as we were on an exit ramp to get to a country side road, a red dually diesel pickup pulled up beside us. The driver honked. The passenger then rolled down his window and shot us the finger while the driver pushed in his clutch and blew black diesel all over me. All I wanted was to get the hell out of Missouri.

Bessie caught up with Shadow about ten miles outside of Jefferson City and the RV crew was not yet aware I had been struck by the "Show Me State" idiot Missouri driver. I kept riding while Conice's crew moved to Shadow, relieving Joe and crew.

Joe took a long walk by himself, trying to put all of this into perspective. He had just witnessed his brother being assaulted with a deadly weapon. *This is just a bicycle race you know! Is it worth the risk? We still have over 1000 miles to go. What happens next?*

Anika and Damaris consoled Joni. This was Joni's first chance to actually let loose since the incident. Everything had happened so quickly back in Jefferson City that she now could actually step back and think about it all. Tears flooded her eyes and her chest heaved as she wept—it was all hitting her now.

I don't think Em ever fully recovered. She just wasn't the same afterwards. Sure, she would eventually get back in her rotation as driver and, of course, she remained stalwart with her determination to get me to Annapolis, but she just wasn't her jovial, enthusiastic self. She wasn't the diehard Rocker Em that I had grown to love. That Missouri driver may have been aiming at me, but I wasn't the only one he hit! Damn him!

There was nothing to be done but to go back to racing RAAM again; I had to stay focused and put all of it behind me. I became extremely exhausted after the adrenaline rush of the hit-and-run incident wore off and, once again, I was having a hard time staying awake, weaving along the edge of the road.

Conice tried hard to keep me awake, with *Running on Empty* by Jackson Browne blaring on my sound system. As he drove, Michael was so pissed off about what had happened that he wasn't letting any cars close to me at all. They could wait in hell as far as he was concerned.

I caught myself dozing off on the bike a couple of times and recognized exactly what was happening. I have always had trouble staying awake when I drive. I have had three auto wrecks in my life and I fell asleep at the wheel in all three. I get so sleepy when I drive that I think to myself, *It would feel so good if I could just close my eyes for three or four seconds.* And so I do close them. Then I open them and when I see that I'm still going straight down the road, I think to myself, *Hmm, that felt good. I think I'll do that again.* After I do that several times I usually fall completely asleep at the wheel. I then just find a pulloff and take a power nap to be on the safe side.

Even though it was in the middle of the afternoon, I finally dozed off one too many times until I eventually woke up lying on the ground. Conice said he saw me weave and then just head straight off the road. Luckily I landed in some thick grass and I wasn't injured. At least it woke me up for a while, so I continued riding.

We crossed the Missouri River near Hermann, Missouri and moved into challenging terrain, with climb after climb over long rolling hills. These weren't the Texas Hill Country-type rollers that I was used to;

these rollers were longer and steeper. Also, traffic was getting heavier the closer we got to Washington, Missouri. The highway was crowded with huge diesel farm trucks, John Deere tractors and 18-wheel hopper trucks hauling asphalt and fill dirt. I have never seen so many trucks. The Missouri highways don't have shoulders or climbing lanes on the always-present hills. No wonder the drivers were impatient. They are always waiting to pass trucks or tractors on the hills and now they find themselves behind an idiot on a bicycle with his follow vehicle climbing up the steep inclines at eight mph.

Team Dex arrived TS34. Washington, MO. 1955 miles. 192 RAAM hours.

Elaine and Em had a really good salad with spaghetti waiting for me at the time station in Washington. Pam Wrob, a friend from Del Rio who also had a home nearby met us at the TS. Pam, an addicted Dexan, brought dozens of home-made chocolate chip cookies for me and the crew. Between the spaghetti and the cookies, I stuffed myself.

Now, approaching the 2000-mile point, I was starting to experience some fairly serious pain and weakness in my hands. My palms were tender from all the pressure I had put on them as I stood up to climb. I was already double gloving, but Dan suggested I also use double tape on my handle bars. Pam went to a local bike shop and bought more tape for the job.

I crossed the Missouri River once more and we soon found ourselves in five o'clock rush hour traffic. Again, the road was two lanes wide with no shoulder, this time with short, even steeper, climbs of 12-15% grade. Traffic was really getting pissed off at us. One man, with a scowl on his face, was even standing out in his yard yelling at us: "Get off the road. You are not welcome here!" He had propped up a huge cardboard sign that said, "Road Not Safe for Cyclists!" This was definitely one of the most stressful sections of the RAAM route.

Of course, nature always calls after a good meal and I soon needed to take another dump, but there was no way I could ever stop on the side of the road in this area. The traffic and congestion was just too great. Dan was in Shadow and he phoned Joni who was in Bessie, still back at the TS. Joni told him they would try to catch us to bring the restroom to me.

Soon after that, I spotted a John Deere tractor dealership on the right side of the road. It looked more like a huge car dealership and, it suddenly dawned on me, *every dealership has a restroom!*

Without even letting Dan know or getting his opinion, I pulled into the JD store. I was desperate—I needed to go and I needed to go NOW! I walked in, clad in sweat-stained jersey and spandex. I stank like road kill, my beard was grey and stubbly, and I had a bad case of helmet hair. My cleated shoes clicked and clacked across the tile floor. Elaine was right behind me, carrying all my dump and saddle sore paraphernalia: latex gloves, Lanacaine, Lantiseptic and Dermablast. She walked right up to a salesman at a desk and asked, "May we use your restroom?"

He looked at her like he was seeing an alien from another planet and didn't say a word. He just pointed over to a corner. He was even more surprised when he saw Elaine follow me into the restroom.

Bessie and crew arrived at the store before I finished my business. Joni entered the store and, without even asking the salesman, went straight to the restroom. Now the salesman knew that we had a threesome in the male john! I quickly finished my business and then, like a little two-year-old boy learning potty training, I looked at Elaine and exclaimed jokingly, "Mommy, I fru! Wipe me!"

Joni doctored my butt and helped me get my three layers of shorts pulled back up. All three of us exited the bathroom and said to the salesman, "Thank you."

He replied rudely, "Whatever!" I'm sure he was close to calling security.

Joni was thinking to herself; *Just get me out of this state and away from these people!*

We were now closing on our next major objective, the Mississippi River, the second of the mandatory time cut-off stations. Volunteers at the previous time station in Washington had given us information about an upcoming detour near the river due to road construction and Dan had called the War Room to get specific instructions.

Sure enough, when we finally arrived at the detour we found the road to be completely impassable due to flood damage. A waiting RAAM official explained that my bike and I would have to be put in our van while the official escorted us through the construction area. While Dan placed my bike in Shadow, Elaine took off my helmet and shoes. This was an opportunity for me to catch a 10-minute nap, so I crawled up onto my foam bed to sleep while the escort vehicle led us along a freeway for about 15 miles. RAAM rules had required all big RVs—this meant Bessie, of course—to take an alternate route or it would have meant a time penalty had RAAM officials seen Bessie on the actual route at this point.

Bessie went on ahead via the required routing and parked several blocks from the end point of the detour. Her entire crew was waiting in the parking lot of the strip mall to greet me and cheer when the RAAM escort vehicle and Shadow arrived. And, wow, did they ever! Joni was dressed in her high school cheerleading uniform complete with pom-pons and she was wearing her oversized orange glasses. Damaris was wearing a multi-colored afro-style wig. Em was carrying a sign that read, "Go, Dex, Go!" and Joe held up a sign that said, "It never always gets worse!" The RAAM official that had escorted us to the restart point was quite impressed by the way the crew was cheering me on.

There was a bicycle shop in this same strip mall and the owner of the shop came out to greet us. He had heard of my incident in Jefferson City and apologized for the rudeness of the Missouri drivers. He admitted he was very aware of the rudeness of Missouri traffic and apologized to us for their actions. He also added that he was part of a coalition to try to educate drivers and the public about sharing the road with cyclists. I thanked him for coming out while at the same time thinking to myself, *good luck with that!*

Team Dex arrived TS35. The Mississippi River. 2028 miles. 198 RAAM hours.

Jackie Griffen: "Dex, you should have been a Navy Seal. I am quite sure that at a younger age you would have qualified."

Sherry Pomroy: "Right after radiation this morning, I checked on you Dex. We can beat these challenges, Amen? Keep pedaling brudda. Chin up, Joni. Prayers going out to the team."

Dan Diaz: "Dex!!! I bet you can almost see the horizon in Maryland. Face ahead, no way home but East. I am in awe!"

Emile Abbot: "Our thoughts are with you all on Team Dex and we know you are sharing the stress along with Dex. Keep up the good work; you guys and gals are great. Rock on as Dex peddles forward."

Stacy Tooke: "Dex, you're Awesome. You have an excellent crew and the Heart of a Warrior. Nothing stopping you now. Stay Strong. Our prayers are with you."

Kat Manton: "Keep on it, Dex. You are a ROCK STAR! Oh wait, that's too punky for you :)—You Rock! All of this is an amazing feat, no matter the outcome. Blessings and strength and courage to you. Love, Kat."

Chapter 10

NO SLEEP FOR OLD MEN

Time Station 35, at the Mississippi River, was the second mandatory time cut-off point—and I made it with a little over six hours to spare. I now had the right to race to the finish line.

I stopped briefly at TS35 to inhale my favorite fried egg sandwich which Elaine made with double cheddar cheese and eggs just sunny-side up enough that, when I bit into them, the yellow ran down my cheeks—exactly like I like 'em!

While I was at the time station, Janet Christiansen's crew chief came over and told me that Janet wanted me to know she was pulling for me. That really meant a lot to me. Janet and I shared similar demons as we both DNFed in Maryland our rookie years. Like me, she had returned to conquer RAAM her sophomore year. Janet knew the physical, psychological and emotional road that lay ahead of me over the next 1000 miles. Unfortunately, Janet had to DNF this year at TS5 in Salome, Arizona due to a knee injury. Her crew chief and staff were following the race as they made their way to the Annapolis finish line.

With Illinois awaiting us on the other side of the Mississippi River, Joe made the now traditional and obligatory announcement over the PA, "Missouri, DONE!" And everyone cheered!

I may have had a little time in the bank, but I was extremely tired. The eight accumulated days of sleep deprivation were really starting to take their toll on me. I hadn't ridden more than about 20 miles into Illinois when I was weaving so badly on the road that Joe and Joni decided to put me down. They thought if I just took a 20-minute power nap that maybe I would wake up and get several more hours riding before I went down for a longer sleep.

I pulled off the road onto a gravel lane that led to an abandoned barn. Joe took my bike, Em helped Joni get my helmet and shoes off, and I climbed into my little crawl space and slept hard. Joni woke me up 20 minutes later and I staggered like a drunk as I tried to make my way over to my bike. I clipped into one pedal and pushed off through some loose rocks on the side of the road. I was so uncoordinated that I crashed before I could clip into the other pedal and I went down hard on the gravel, scraping my elbow and slamming the back of my head on the ground as I fell. I had landed on my right hip and I could feel raw skin under my shorts from the fall.

Joni immediately declared, "That's it. You are not going any further without a good sleep!"

She put me back in the van for a two-hour nap. When I awoke, she had to go through the same routine she always did after one of my sleeps. She had to answer my questions about where I was and what I was doing; I had no clue of either. After about an hour of riding, though, I started to get my wits about me.

Em took over the PA system and, to keep me awake, she began to talk to me about an imaginary movie she thought would be a blockbuster. She decided that Team Dex ought to send a screenplay to Tom Hanks so he could make a film about us. She said it would be a huge hit because of all the Dexans who were following us online. It got us all to talking and discussing the idea with Joe and Joni joining in on the charade to give their two cents worth.

Em decided she would be the casting director for the movie. The picture naturally needed a knock-out diva as leading lady and Em decided that would, of course, be her character and she cast Julia Roberts to play that role. The leading lady would most certainly need a hunk for a romantic interlude and Em decided that would be my brother Joe, to be played by Matthew McConaughey. Then, she needed a veteran actor, (notice how I said "veteran" instead of old) to play the part of me. People have said I look somewhat like Ed Harris, so Ed got the nod for my role. I sure hoped the guy could ride a bike!

Then the rest of the casting started to flow. Em couldn't decide whether to fill Michael's role with Justin Bartha, who played the IT guru in *National Treasure*, or Richard Dean Anderson from the *MacGyver* series. Kathy Bates was a shoo-in for Elaine with her charismatic love of life and her captivating sense of humor. Because of his high energy, the role of Conice would be played by Jim Carrie. For Anika, Em needed a young, upcoming actress so we decided Shelbie Bruce, the young star in *Spanglish*, would fill that role. Due to her sociable personality and contagious smile, Damaris' character could only be filled by Oprah Winfrey. I suggested Sally Field for Joni but she got all pissed off about that saying that if Meg Ryan didn't play her, then she wasn't going to be involved with the film at all. Then there was Dan. With his flaming red hair and comedic skills, Will Ferrel would fit the bill there. Of course every movie needs a villain, so Em decided that the Team Dex webmaster, Michael Tarbet, would be the corporate executive type who plots to sabotage the entire race and end Dex's RAAM dream. Who else to better play Michael Tarbet than *Wall Street* villain Michael Douglas?

I told her the theme of the movie shouldn't necessarily be about RAAM or Team Dex. The theme of the film should be about America and how the entire country gets involved with the inspiring story of a simple, small-town, West Texas guy's battle with the toughest bike race on the planet: the Beast known as RAAM. For two weeks, everyone all across the country becomes addicted to their computers as they follow him online. America is hooked, desperate to find out if an over-60, former couch potato and heavy smoker could cross America in 12 days on a bicycle without suffering permanent psychological or physical damage. But then Em ran into the same problem every other movie producer seems to run into: no budget. So much for *No Sleep for Old Men*.

Team Dex arrived TS36. Greenville, IL. 2074 miles. 205 RAAM hours.

Aristotle wrote, "We are what we repeatedly do. Excellence then, is not an act, but a habit." I have my own similar approach and I call it my 21-day Rut Theory. The idea is that we are all creatures of habit and all it takes to form a "rut" is to do something for 21 consecutive days. Some ruts are good, some are bad but, either way, if you do something for 21 consecutive days without fail, sure enough, you will form a rut.

To give you a simple example, suppose upon waking up every morning of your life you have been putting your right leg into your pants first—that is a rut. Do you know what will happen if you wake up the next morning and try putting your pants on by placing your left leg into your pants first? That's right, you will fall flat on your butt! However, if you get up every morning for the next 21 mornings in a row and put your left leg in first, then you will form a new rut. And do you know what will happen if, on the 22nd day, you try to put your right leg in first? That's right, you will fall flat on your butt!

So when people ask me how to start an exercise program or how to lose weight or how to run or how to ride a bike, I tell everyone of them that all it takes is consistency. It is as simple as that. All anyone has to do is form their rut and stick with it.

I remember one day I was riding on one of the National Park Service roads on Lake Amistad near my home when I met a NPS suburban coming my way. The Ranger slowed the truck as he approached and stuck his arm out the window indicating he wanted me to stop. I recognized the Ranger as I had seen him out there for years.

He told me, "Dex, I just want to let you know that you won't be seeing me around anymore. I am retiring and this is my last week on the job. You know, Dex, I started working for the National Park Service 20 years ago and the very first day I was on the job I saw you riding your bike on this very same road and I have continued to see you throughout my entire career. I just want you to know it has been a pleasure."

All it takes is consistency, people!

The sun still hadn't risen when I departed Greenville, Illinois. Conice's crew was back on duty in Shadow and Conice, being the medic he was, immediately got on the headset and started through his patient assessment: "Dex, how are you feeling?"

"I'm feeling wonderful Conice. I feel like I could ride for days!" I responded. *Yeah, like I believe that!*

Conice continued with his list of questions: "How are your saddle sores?"

"I haven't changed my shorts since I left the Mississippi. I'll need some fresh ones soon."

"How about your elbows?"

"As long as my padding doesn't slip down, the elbows are okay."

"How are your hands doing?"

"My palms are bruised and tender. I keep moving my hand position on my handle bars and I can't stay in one position for more than 30 seconds or so. When I stand to climb, the pressure on my hands is really painful."

"How is your shoulder doing? How are the strawberries on your elbow and hip from the crash?"

"My shoulder just feels tight. Not painful. I can feel the raw skin on my hip from the crash. But it isn't any worse than the raw skin from my saddle sores."

"Let's do a head to toe assessment now."

"Let's not! Turn up the music. I could use some Van Halen about now!"

Finally, the sun popped its head over the eastern horizon and I felt like I would soon perk up. True to the nature of RAAM, just about the time I was getting into a groove, traffic up ahead came to an abrupt stop. Apparently there was construction and the road was closed and we had to wait for a pilot car to lead us down the single lane.

Michael got on the PA and wisely explained to me, "There are two seasons in the Northeast: winter and construction. It takes a whole season of construction to repair the road damage from the winter!"

With mock cheer, I replied, "Whoopee! Now I have a lot to look forward to!"

The elevation between Greenville and Effingham, Illinois didn't vary more than 250 feet but it was a constant up and down on short rollers—the kind of riding I do best. I could attack each uphill and then use my momentum on each downhill to the best of my advantage to get me up the other side. I was making some good time considering I had been in the saddle for over 2000 miles.

Team Dex arrived TS37. Effingham, IL. 2123 miles. 209 RAAM hours.

It was close to 8:00 a.m. local time when I left Effingham. The temperature was in the low 70s and I had a slight tailwind—perfect conditions. Perfect, that is, except for the construction. What made the construction worse was the hundreds of 18-wheel hopper trucks hauling new dirt in or taking old dirt out as they replaced the pavement. I had never seen so many trucks in my life. I hoped these people up here would never discover the wide open spaces in Texas and all decide to move.

It was here that Dan nearly screwed up big time. We were coming up to two dams and we were supposed to stay to the right as we approached one of them, then veer east away from the other. Dan couldn't keep his damn DAMS straight and I veered when I was supposed to stay to the right. Fortunately, Damaris quickly caught the mistake and had me back on track before too much damage was done. Elaine called it Dan's "boo boo." This reminded me of an anecdote.

Over the microphone I asked for Elaine on the headset. She was always a great sport and good for a laugh and I needed one about now.

I asked, "Hey Elaine, did you ever tell Damaris about your boob catch?"

I heard Damaris exclaim in the background, "Her what!?"

So then I told Damaris the entire story. We were on a 500-mile training ride one weekend and Dan had flown down from Boulder, Colorado just to get in some crewing practice, so it was the first time Elaine and Dan had worked together. I was about 200 miles into the ride, somewhere between Big Lake and Rankin out in west Texas, and I had just finished off a flask of Perpetuem. Dan was in the navigator position and I told him via the headset that they could pull up beside me and I would hand off the empty container. Joni was driving, so she pulled Shadow alongside. Elaine, in the back seat, was the domestique and she was hanging out the side window with her arms and hands extended, reaching for the flask. Being a little top heavy, so to speak, this wasn't the easiest thing in the world for Elaine to do so, instead of handing the flask to her like I should have, I decided I would toss it to her. She tried to catch it with her hands, but instead she caught it right in the center of her ample cleavage. From then on, an empty flask hand-off was referred to as an "Elaine Boob Catch."

Damaris got a big kick out of it, but sharp-tongued and witty Elaine came back with a mock threat: "You will pay for that one, Princess!"

I was prepared for just such a response, though. "Oh yeah?" I said. "Then how about the time we were on that training ride to Sanderson? You were domestique. We were out in the middle of nowhere. It was just before dawn and I had stopped to take a leak. You decided you needed to go also but you were too skiddish to walk out into the tall grass in the dark and squat. So you elected to squat right there on the pavement in front of Shadow's headlights—but, you had forgotten Mauro, my IT guy at work, had installed a video camera on the dash of the van that was videoing the entire ride. None of us even thought about it until later when we were watching the video and saw you out there in all your glory."

Elaine shouted angrily into the microphone, "You better not ever put that on YouTube!"

I just laughed and said, "Gotcha!"

We crossed the Wabash River and were now in Indiana where local time and RAAM time were finally the same. Dan yelled out on the PA system, "Illinois, DONE!"

Bessie was already up ahead at TS38 in Sullivan waiting for us. Here, another tiny RAAM moment played itself out while I was out on the road. There was a Krispy Kreme Donut Shop near the station, so Joe went over and bought two dozen super-glazed, mouth-watering, sugar-spiking, Krispy Kremes for Team Dex. Then he looked across the intersection and noticed Kathy-Roche Wallace, just standing there, straddling her bike. He didn't see her crew, so Joe walked over and asked, "How are you doing Kathy?"

She had a far-away gaze in her eyes and her mouth was gaped open. She turned her head slightly toward Joe and replied, "Uuuuugh."

Joe said, "You are doing great!"

Kathy once again replied, "Uuuuugh."

"Where's your crew?"

Kathy once again mouthed as she shrugged her shoulders, "Uuuuugh."

Joe lifted the box of Krispy Kreme donuts and asked, "Would you like a donut?"

Kathy's eyes lit up. She nodded and said, "Uuuuuuh, huuuuuh."

Joe handed her a donut and she scarfed it down. She didn't hesitate to lick every bit of icing off her dirty fingers.

"Would you like another"?

Almost before he could get the words out, Kathy reached into the box and grabbed another Krispy.

Much later, at the RAAM awards banquet in Annapolis, Team Dex was sitting at their crew table when Kathy walked over and said, "I don't know when or where, but somebody from this table gave me a Krispy Kreme during RAAM. That was the best donut I have ever eaten!"

Team Dex arrived TS38. Sullivan, IN. 2196 miles. 216 RAAM hours.

More construction. More congested traffic. Gosh dang it! At mile 12 out of Sullivan, I had to once again wait for a pilot vehicle to lead me through the construction. The line of traffic waiting must have been over a mile long and all those people behind me were going to be even more pissed off because they would soon have to drive 15 mph behind me going through the single lane road.

At about mile marker 40 we hit some short mountain grades with lots of turns and, all of a sudden, the route got much bumpier. It was somewhere in this section that Kirk Gentle passed me—the only other Texan in this year's RAAM besides me. In the entire history of RAAM, there have only been five solo finishers from Texas and we both were aiming to change that. Like me, Kirk was returning for his second attempt at RAAM after DNFing his rookie year.

Kirk and I had raced together back in September of 2010 at the Texas Time Trials. We had taken first and second place with Kirk on top. He was all smiles as he passed me there in Indiana, telling me, "I've got the best looking gals in RAAM for my support crew. Let them know if you need anything at all. They will be happy to help!" Then he gave me an evil grin.

The road continued with two lanes, no shoulder and a double yellow stripe indicating no passing most of the time, and the traffic was horrendous. Michael, up ahead in Bessie, in order to miss some of the traffic, had decided to take an alternate route to Bloomington. On the RAAM course, the closer we got to Bloomington, the worse the traffic became. Once in town, Joe pointed out the Indiana University stadium as I rode by. Maybe I was in some kind of euphoric state, but I must say that even though the traffic was horrible, Indiana was one of my favorite states—the rolling hills were green and pretty, and the houses were definitely models of Americana. All the picket fences seemed to have a fresh coat of white paint and the yards were groomed. Furthermore, I don't think I ever saw one driver shoot me the finger in the entire state.

My legs hurt, my bones hurt, my elbows hurt, my hands hurt, my feet hurt, my butt hurt. I had mouth sores and my tongue was so swollen that I had to just mumble my words.

I was straddling my bike at an intersection in Hutsonville, Indiana waiting for the red light to turn green when I looked across the intersection at a guy on a motorcycle as he also waited for the light. I thought to myself, *Look at that guy. He is normal. He isn't tired. He isn't sleep deprived. He is living a normal life. He is going to ride his little motorcycle home tonight and he is going to eat a good supper, take a hot shower and then go to bed. Why can't I take a shower? Why can't I just lie down and feel that soft white sheet as it floats down over my skin? People take showers every day. People sleep every day. Hell, some people even take naps in the middle of the day. Why can't I be like some people? Why can't I be normal?*

Team Dex arrived TS39. Bloomington, IN. 2263 miles. 223 RAAM hours.

It was a little past 10:00 p.m. when I departed TS39. In Shadow, Conice and crew followed me out of the CVS Pharmacy parking lot back onto the route. Navigation was tricky here as I still had several turns before getting out of the busy city. I had just passed a Circle K store and then took an immediate right turn onto a street lined with low, overhanging trees. Michael was blocking for me, staying as close as possible to my rear wheel. Unfortunately, in his concentration, he had forgotten about my back-up bicycle on the roof of Shadow and he had driven right through some of the lower branches. I heard Conice yell on the PA, "Stop Dex. We need to stop!"

Michael jumped out of Shadow to inspect the damage. He looked everything over with a flashlight as best he could. The 20-year-old Trek 1400 seemed okay and the high dollar spare carbon tubular wheels still had all their spokes, so we pushed on.

I only rode for about another hour before I was so sleepy I couldn't keep my head up. The headlights from Shadow would reflect into the rear view mirror on my helmet and the instant bright reflection in the dark looked more like a lightening bolt to me so I thought there was a storm behind me. I was once again weaving on the dark highway, talking with my hallucinatory friends. Billy Box, a Crane High School buddy I hadn't seen in a couple of decades, was riding with me. I asked him, "How far back is the storm? Have you ever been struck by lightening?"

Of course Conice could hear me through the headset but had no idea I was talking to my imaginary friend, not him. Conice replied, "There is no lightening or storm Dex. Just ride your bike. You are fine!"

Anika, though, understood that I was hallucinating and, very shortly, Conice told me to pull over at the next wide spot. He was going to put me down. I found a place to pull over, but nearly fell off my bike as I was too weak and uncoordinated to unclip from my pedals. As Anika helped me remove my helmet and shoes, her eyes revealed pity for this scrungy old man. She had this sad look on her face that seemed to say, *I'm so sorry you are hurting so much. I wish I could make it all better.*

Anika was the only crew member on Team Dex who had no knowledge of my RAAM 2010. She didn't ride a bike and she had never even heard the word RAAM until November of 2010. Anika was the newest elementary art teacher in the school district and looked to Joni as a mentor. A very independent, talented, capable, young woman she was beginning a second career in teaching after a first career as a graphic designer—a job she lost when the economy collapsed a few years ago. Joni had the opportunity to get to know Anika in November when they roomed together at the 2010 Texas Art Teachers Association art conference in Austin. At the time all Joni could talk about was RAAM. Anika was impressed with the whole concept of riding a bicycle across the country, and became fascinated with the idea as Joni shared with her the adventure stories.

As Joni began making plans to go back to RAAM in 2011, Anika asked how things were going. Joni told her of the need for more crew members, and quickly thought to herself; *Hmmm . . . here is a twenty-seven year old, single teacher.* So, before Anika could get away from her, Joni asked her if she would consider joining the crew. Being the adventurous type, Anika's response was, "Sure, why not?" Joni told her that I would have to meet her, so we set up a dinner date at Chili's the following evening. As usual I painted the bleakest picture of RAAM that I could, but this did not seem to spook Anika. She simply reasoned that now was the time to participate in such an adventure, since she was unattached and had the summer off. So, she became our second domestique, and had to learn how to take care of me during the training rides. She signed up for two such rides and quickly picked up the skill of hanging out of the van window to hand off flasks of Perpetuem. Her energy was a great asset to the crew and everyone seemed to adopt her as "the little sister." Being so much younger than everyone else, we were surprised at how she just fit right in with the rest of the crew. Joni believed Anika's strongest trait was her adaptable and congenial teacher personality.

I slept for two hours in my little crawl space in Shadow while Conice, Michael and Anika stood outside in the dark so as to not disturb me. Anika apologized as she woke me: "I'm so sorry Dex, but you have to get up." She answered my questions before I could even ask: "You are in a bicycle race. It is the Race Across America. It is time for you to ride your bike."

Right before I had gone down for my sleep, Conice had been playing *All My Life's a Circle* by Harry Chapin, one of my favorite story tellers—I have all of his songs in my music collection. *Circle* continued to play in my head as I pedaled through the night:

> *"All my life's a circle, sunrise and sundown,*
> *The moon rolls through the nighttime, 'til the daybreak comes around.*
> *All my life's a circle, and I can't tell you why,*
> *The seasons spinning by again,*
> *The years keep rollin' by.*
> *And the years keep rollin' by."*

The lyrics were certainly appropriate; the years were sure rolling by in this old man's life.

Team Dex arrived TS40. Greensburg, IN. 2326 miles. 232 RAAM hours.

Carl Svajda: "Dex, you are leaving me speechless, which all you Tooke's know is difficult. You are in our prayers. Keep up the amazing and astounding work."

Diana Arreola: "We too have been checking on you every day since you started, sometimes five and six times a day, and we have also been praying for you and your crew because the 5 O'clock Rockers are part of your crew, too. We have been running on Veteran's Blvd. on Tuesdays and Thursdays and scream and yell when we pass the Bank & Trust when we see your name and how many miles you have completed. And tell Joni that we have been moving Dex on the school bulletin board at Garfield and we show our students where he is on the map and the miles completed. Go, Dex, Go!!!!!!! You are our hometown and Texas HERO and an inspiration to all of us."

Ken Austin: "Dex, sorry about the Hoosier Hi-Winds through our great state. I wish that didn't happen. Praying for you here at Garcor Supply. Bob and I say, 'Hey, good luck and keep up the great work.' Seems your time is great. But don't let that fool you. Keep slammin' those pedals to the finish. God speed and God bless you Dex . . . Be safe . . . You are truly an inspiration to us and you are truly an awesome man. Ken and Bob @ Garcor Supply, Franklin, Indiana."

Tim Culpepper: "Have been following you every day since you started. Our prayers are with you and your crew. Find a way to keep your motivation up and keep your sights on the FINISH LINE. You are living my dream of one day being an Official RAAM Finisher."

Brenda Beard: "Dex is a lean, mean, pedaling machine!!!! Keep it going. Can you smell that finish line???"

Avery Grace: "I don't have a Facebook account. I'm on my Dad's. Good job. How far you are right now? Good luck."

Mike Wrob: "Dex, can you smell that? It's the finish line! This is your strongest part of the race. The victory party is waiting."

Dan Joder
aka Delilah, queen of sappy love songs

Michael West and Anika, with Dex

Crew huddle prior to the Pre-Race Inspection.

The "Before" Shot--Elaine and Emily

Joni and Dex..Crew Chief and Racer

Photo: Daniel Joder

Dex at work in Arizona,
about 650 miles into RAAM

Photo: Daniel Joder

Dex on Day 10

Team Dex Crew for RAAM 2011

Top row, L to R: Conice, Damaris, Anika, Michael T., Emily
Bottom row, L to R: Dan, Joni, Joe, Elaine, Michael W.

Dexans and the Orange Glasses Craze

Joe gives Dex instructions at the Durango TS.

Team Dex celebrates at the summit of Wolf Creek Pass, 938 miles into RAAM

A smile for Sideling Hill, Maryland,
2,802 miles into RAAM

Finish Line Celebration,
Conice and Damaris

Joni and Dex Tooke--and the famous orange glasses!

The business is finished!

Photo: Joe Tooke

TO ANNAPOLIS, MD · 3000 MILES

RACE ACROSS

Dex Tooke – Solo RAAM
12 days 19 hours 46 minutes

Chapter 11

THE MAGIC NUMBER 10

Greensville, Greensburg, Greendale, I don't know where the hell I am. It seems like every other town I come to has "Green" in the name. Why does every state have to have a town named Green? Gosh dang it! My brain is mush. I'm having a hard time figuring out whether the thoughts in my head are actual thoughts or hallucinations. I can't tell the difference. Maybe there is no difference. I guess I didn't do enough "head game" training rides in preparation.

As I think I've made clear by now, RAAM is as much mental as it is physical. I knew this from 2010 so, while preparing for 2011, I did what I called "head game" training rides. These rides were designed to prepare my head, not just my legs as I knew RAAM was going to offer up plenty of psychological battles.

To give an example of what I mean, on one particular day, after being awake since 4:00 a.m., I waited until 6:00 p.m. to start my head game ride. I then rode 180 miles from 6:00 p.m. until 6:00 a.m. the next morning. I rode in the dark, starting out when I was already tired, and the big kicker was that I did the entire 180 miles on a three mile out and back route. Every three miles I would do a 180-degree turn-around—I never left the same three miles. You talk about boring! You talk about head games! You can't even imagine the thoughts that went through my mind and the tricks my psyche tried to play on me. But, I felt it was a very necessary part of my RAAM training.

Delilah, the radio queen of sappy love songs—that is, Dan and crew—was back manning Shadow. Dan got on the headset and told me Cathy Gearheart, the TS41 captain, had just phoned and she didn't know if she was going to be able to get to the Oxford TS in time to greet Team Dex or not. Cathy was a photographer and big Dexan fan carrying over from 2010. She had taken some great photos of me as I passed through

Oxford last year. I told Dan to tell her I would be disappointed if I missed her, but I totally understood.

The first 15 miles or so heading out of whatever "Green" town I was in was clogged with heavy traffic. Finally, though, I emerged into the countryside with some nice rolling hills and pretty green scenery. The temperature was in the mid 60s and I had a slight tailwind as I passed through Oldenburg, Indiana. Jerome, Arizona was probably my favorite town in the west, but so far Oldenburg was leading the pack in the east.

The countryside was a constant, deep, lush green as I followed the curvy road. One mile we would pass through beautiful green forests and then the next mile would find ourselves in pretty green pastures with plenty of dairy cows for me to "MOO COW" to. There was a light drizzle but it was never wet enough to saturate my jersey or shorts.

Through this section I was feeling a little perky. In fact, I was feeling so perky that Elaine actually was able to do a moving Ensure flask hand-off from the van. I hadn't had enough coordination for something like that in days!

Soon after, I passed through a small town named Mixerville and I heard Dan shout over the PA system, "Indiana, DONE! We were now in Ohio! Eight states down!" I wondered to myself, *how long had it taken for Dan to figure out how many states we had been through?*

Once in Ohio, it didn't take long to notice the state's enthusiasm for RAAM. There were RAAM route markers spaced regularly along almost the entire route. The volunteers at TS41 in Oxford, Ohio had done a tremendous job of posting these wonderful markers which read, "Caution! Bike Route. Race Across America."

There were several turns and curves leading into Oxford, the home of Miami University and the college students were enjoying their summer vacation. One young guy, standing on the balcony of his upstairs apartment, even yelled out, "Go, RAAM!" as I passed by.

College students party, right? Isn't college all about partying? Well, sure enough, it wasn't even noon yet and I saw a group of a half-dozen students playing beer pong in the front yard of their apartment dorm. They all cheered and yelled when they saw Team Dex come rolling through their town. *Now why couldn't I be playing beer pong instead of seeing if I could set the world record for saddle sores?*

Dex Tooke

Team Dex arrived TS41. Oxford, OH. 2376 miles. 237 RAAM hours.

The Oxford TS was another of the fully-manned time stations in RAAM and there was a flurry of activity there as we arrived. It was a pleasant surprise to find Amy and John McFaddin there, two of my best friends from RAAM 2010. Amy and John were TS captains at Blanchester, Ohio but spent a lot of time volunteering at both Oxford and Blanchester.

Em and Anika had cooked some spaghetti on the RV stove top, so I stepped into Bessie to eat, inviting Amy and John to visit with me while I munched away. They brought several photo posters of me from 2010 and asked if I would autograph them so they could later give them away as souvenirs at the time station. It was wonderful to see and talk with them again.

Then, Amy presented a gift to me: a framed photo that had been shot at the very start of RAAM this year, barely ten days ago. It showed me coming up the steep climb leading away from the beach at Oceanside. Wow, did that seem like a lifetime ago! I looked so fresh and clean—no grey, stubbly beard, no sun-scorched face or blisters. I looked like a real cyclist; not at all like I looked now.

Dave Elsberry, one of my 60-plus compatriots, was at Oxford when we got ready to depart. His crew wasn't around and he said he wasn't sure where they were. He had no idea how to get out of town or the route to follow, so he asked if he could tag along with us until his crew caught up. I told him, "Sure, as long as you can ride as slow as me." We hadn't even gotten out of Oxford before his crew showed up and Dave left me behind.

As I went through Trenton, about 10 miles outside of Oxford, a young kid on a 20" bike started chasing me. He eventually caught then passed me. Joe got on the PA system and yelled at the kid, "Go ride 2500 miles and then come back and try that!"

The kid slowed after he passed me, so I rode up beside him and explained to him about RAAM. The kid asked, "Are you riding for a cause?"

I didn't have the time or mental capacity to explain to him about BCFS, so I said, "Yeah, I'm riding for a cause. 'Cause I want to!"

The route was taking me directly between Cincinnati and Dayton, Ohio, two large population centers, so the traffic was heavy, and the pavement was wet from a light rain. Behind me in Shadow, Em was driving and blocking as best she could while I just tried to stay focused enough not to get run over.

Through this area, Joe was calling the turns over the PA system and, at one point, told me I had a surprise coming up in about three miles. I had no idea what he was talking about but, shortly after that, as I was riding through some construction near I-75, Joe told me to pull over and stop at a wide spot up ahead. It was muddy where I stopped and I nearly fell down. Joe came over to me after I stopped and pointed across the highway to a truck parked on the opposite side of the road. There was a man standing in front of the truck and he started to walk toward me. Joe asked, "You know who that is?"

My eyes were so tired and my vision so poor that I could barely see him. Joe said, "That is Mario Casas, Mayte's husband."

I couldn't believe it. Mario and Mayte were close friends from Del Rio and both were instrumental in the success of the BCFS fund-raising committee, my designated RAAM charity. Mario's work required a lot of traveling and he happened to be working in Dayton. He had been following Team Dex online, so he knew where I was along the route. I got a lump in my throat as I gave Mario a big hug. It really meant a lot to me for him to make the effort to come out and find me. The idea that I had so many people supporting me and cheering me on was very motivating.

The visit was brief and I was quickly back on the busy road. My hands were hurting and I was having trouble with my bike—the gears weren't shifting properly. I presumed it was because they were caked in mud and grime.

The rain was just hard enough to make the road dangerously slick and mess up my glasses so I finally had to remove them. My vision had already begun to get blurry even with my glasses. Without my glasses, though, my vision was even more blurry and I started to have vertigo issues. Joni put some moistening eye drops in both eyes. She knew from experience what happens once my eyes dry out.

I had been racing in the Texas Hill Country 600 in 2010 prior to RAAM that year and was about 325 miles into the race, riding through wet and foggy conditions in the wee hours of the night. I had stopped to wipe the fog off my glasses, then 10 minutes later I had to stop to wipe my glasses again. It didn't seem to matter if I wiped my glasses or not, I couldn't get the fog off the lenses. It was then that I figured out my glasses weren't fogging up at all; it was my vision that was foggy because my eyes had dried out. By the time the sun came up, my vision was so blurry that I couldn't make out the fog line on the road. I could only see large objects, like cars. I finished the race and we immediately went to Walgreens to buy some drops. It took several hours for my vision to finally clear. Lesson learned—and Joni wasn't going to let that happen again.

Team Dex arrived TS42. Blanchester, OH. 2426 miles. 242 RAAM hours.

I needed to take a dump so I took advantage of the McDonalds at the TS. As usual, Joni got weird looks as she carried all my butt meds and followed this stinky old man into the men's restroom. While I was inside doing my duty, Dan tried to adjust my rear derailleur to correct the shifting problem. He test rode my bike and announced, "It's shifting good now, Dex."

John and Amy had driven up from Oxford and were already at Blanchester when I arrived. Joni needed to do a load of laundry and asked John if there was a nearby Laundromat. John replied, "Sure, at my house."

So, while Shadow and I continued on the RAAM route, Bessie and crew followed John to their house, which he graciously opened up for showers, laundry and a bit of rest. A shower is a rarity in RAAM and is a huge moral builder. Joe was accused of using all the hot water but it was still a wonderful interlude for Bessie's crew. *Oh, how I wish I could have showered!*

John and Amy were huge RAAM fans and their home showed it. John gave the crew a short tour, showing off their RAAM room where they had posters of Jure and Gerhard on the wall. I was honored when I found out that they even had one of me from the 2010 RAAM included in the shrine. To top off the tour, John took Em and Elaine out to his garden where they picked fresh lettuce and tomatoes to take along in Bessie.

On duty behind me in Shadow, Conice's crew missed out on the McFadden hospitality as they were busy trying to get me through more construction while I headed out of Blanchester. The next 50 miles took us through a sector of on-again, off-again construction, with ripped up asphalt. It was difficult enough to ride and navigate through detours and construction during the day, but it became even more arduous once night fell.

I was at a low point. My body had wasted away to nothing and my morale and spirit was practically non-existent. Everything hurt. Every pedal stroke was a chore. I just kept saying to myself, *RFM—Relentless Forward Motion.* The Shadow crew recognized my deteriorating condition so Conice put some of my Rocker music over the sound system in an effort to energize me, but I told him, "Take it off. I don't want to listen to any music!"

"Would you like me to read you some Facebook comments?"

"No, I don't want to hear anything. Just leave me alone!"

I was struggling to hang on. RAAM is all about attitude and you better have the right attitude or it will break you. Once RAAM breaks you mentally, it becomes almost impossible to continue. I was totally lacking the confidence that is absolutely necessary to battle RAAM. I was extremely close to self destruction. *What was I doing here? Who am I? This is insane. What was I thinking about? Whatever made me think I was RAAM material?*

I'm a movie buff—Joni and I go to tons of movies. Either we meet at the theater on Fridays after work, or we have our movie "date" on Saturday afternoons. The only reason I begin my weekly Saturday 100-plus-mile training ride at 4:00 a.m. is so I can get finished in time to have my Saturday afternoon movie date.

I'm a pushover for a romantic comedy and, yes, I go to all the chick flicks. I may play hard rock at my spin class, but my favorite music is movie soundtracks. Nothing relaxes me more than a good John Barry, Hans Zimmer or James Horner soundtrack. For me, it just doesn't get any better than Trevor Jones' soundtrack from *The Last of the Mohicans.*

In films, I always pull for the underdog and my favorite movies are the ones based on real life events where the little guy upsets the champion or catches his dream. I must confess I get a little teary-eyed and a lump forms in my throat every time the hero saves the day or dies trying.

So, as my attitude and spirit were spiraling downward that night, I thought of the movie *Secretariat.* I remembered how Diane Lane's character had taken the risk of picking a foal from the mare Somethingroyal, whose bloodline was made up of many horses with stamina, rather than taking the obvious choice of the foal with the faster genetic history. I thought about the heart displayed by Big Red (Secretariat's nickname) as he won the Triple Crown. Then I thought about the lyrics of the song in the movie, *It's Who You Are*:

> *It's not the price*
> *It's not the game*
> *It's not the score*
> *It's not the fame*
> *Whatever road looks way too far*
> *It's not what you have*
> *It's who you are*
>
> *It's not how fast*
> *It's not how far*
> *It's not of cheers*
> *It's who you are*

It was then that I decided the answer to the unanswerable questions I kept asking myself. It was simple: it's who I am.

I finally arrived in Chillicothe, Ohio at close to midnight and I had to ride through a couple of miles of the city before getting to the actual time station. Over the headset, Conice had been navigating me through several turns. At one point, I was straddling my bike at a "T" intersection while I waited on the red light to change. As I sat at the light, I heard him tell me that I was going to take a right-hand turn. Then, just before the light changed, he said, "Take a left, Dex."

He had been talking through my headset and the battery must have been getting low because I could barely hear him. I hadn't gone but a few blocks when I heard Conice say something, but it was unintelligible, so I asked him to use the PA system instead.

Almost immediately, Conice's voice came out loud and clear over the PA: "Dex, we are going the wrong direction. You need to turn around and head back." Tired, sleepy, and now frustrated, I turned around.

I passed by the "T" intersection again and rode through the downtown area of Chillicothe. Again I heard Conice say, "Dex, we have gone too far, you need to turn around." So I turned around once more. I could tell that Conice and Michael were getting frustrated—it was obvious we were lost.

Conice finally got on the PA again and told me, "Dex, pull over at the McDonalds."

The McDonalds parking lot was practically empty due to the late hour. Anika got out of Shadow, took my bike and leaned it against the brick wall while I collapsed on the outdoor dining table and Michael got on the phone with the crew in Bessie. Apparently Bessie was already at the time station and was trying to give directions to Michael. Conice, with flashlight in hand, was studying the route book. Neither one was instilling much confidence in me at that point.

It was then that I saw a McFlurry poster in one of the McDonalds windows. *Oh, what I would give for a Rolo McFlurry right now.* I had no money so I turned to Anika, gave her my most pitiful look and told her, "I don't have any money. But if you will loan me enough money to buy a McFlurry, I will pay you back later."

It was so good! I cherished every spoonful. I didn't care how long it took Conice and Michael to figure out where we were—I could sit here and eat McFlurries all night long.

Finally, they figured out that I was less than a mile from our goal. I crossed a nearby overpass and like magic, Bessie and the TS appeared.

Team Dex arrived TS43. Chillicothe, OH. 2484 miles. 249 RAAM hours.

Anika helped me remove my helmet and shoes, I crawled into my little space in the van, and I was out before my head hit the foam. Joni recognized my deep exhaustion and she knew I needed more than just a 30-minute power nap, so she decided to put me down for what would be my longest sleep in RAAM: three hours.

When I awoke, Joni led me to Bessie. She medicated my saddle sores and then dressed me just like a mother would dress a two-year-old. I lay on the bed as she instructed me to raise each leg and put it through my short's leg. She had to put my leg warmers on just like she would put her pantyhose on herself. She told me to raise my arms so she could get my jersey over my head. Elaine and Em had two potato and cheese breakfast tacos waiting for me and I drank a Dr. Pepper while I sat down to eat.

Joni had to once again explain to me where I was and what I was doing as I had no idea. Joe and Conice reminded me I needed to get moving; I was losing too much time. I kept stalling, though. I just knew I didn't want to get up from that sofa.

The Shadow crew had swapped out and Dan and crew were back on duty. Sadly, even though Michael had installed what we thought were freshly charged batteries into the headset, it malfunctioned within the first 20 minutes, so not getting to hear Dan's stories made the night even longer. He would come over the PA system every now and then just to see if I was awake, but it just wasn't the same as hearing his Delilah voice through the headset.

I was out of it. Even though I had just gone down for three hours, I was nodding off on the bike. I just couldn't go any further and my hallucinatory friends returned. I guess hallucinating is like dreaming except you are awake. The headlight beam from Shadow reflected in my rear view mirror and the quick flash caused me to look over my left shoulder. Ann, a former paramedic partner, was right there on my shoulder. She kept telling me, "Go faster, go faster!" She used to always tell me that when I was driving the Box (the ambulance) to a scene. She always wanted to go faster. I asked her, "You want to drive?" Then she disappeared just as quickly as she had appeared.

Dan heard my conversation and could tell I was hallucinating. I had ridden less than 25 miles since the last TS and now Dan had to put me down for a 15-minute power nap. It went by in a flash and Elaine woke me up, helped me with my shoes and helmet, put eye drops in my eyes, and we were off once more.

Thankfully, the headset battery was completely charged and working again, so I had convenient conversation with Shadow once more. Elaine came over the speaker and told me she had received a message from Tawana Billeaudeau, a friend of mine who worked at the Bank and Trust. Elaine told me Tawana had taken a group of Girl Scouts to Ft. Davis State Park for a campout. She and several of the Girl Scouts had been following Team Dex online but, where they were camped, there was no internet reception. So, the entire group hiked to the top of a mountain just to get to where they could check the status of Team Dex.

I had been riding for over 10 days now. My low points were becoming more frequent and lasting longer and my high points were fewer and shorter. I was staring the Beast in the eyes once again, just like in 2010. This was gut time. This was when I would really have to dig deep. I needed every ounce and speck of motivation there was in my heart and bones to keep me going.

Solo RAAM is most assuredly a test of one's entire being. It is not just a physical or mental fight. RAAM is a battle of emotions and spirit. I thought to myself, *Jure Robic never rode for 10 days in RAAM. I bet he couldn't do this. I know he was much faster but I bet his effort wasn't any greater than mine. Oh, shut up, you fool. You are just feeling pity for yourself. Remember what Kurt says, "Shut up. Just get on your bike and ride!"*

Team Dex arrived TS44. Athens, OH. 2543 miles. 258 RAAM hours.

There is a magic number in RAAM and that number is 10. Every RAAM racer knows this number; it represents 10 mph. Once a racer falls below the 10 mph mark in RAAM, he is considered doomed. It is the kiss of death. History is not a liar and the history of RAAM shows that very few racers ever finish RAAM once they have fallen below the 10 mph line. Once your average speed begins to drop, it is nearly impossible to bring it back up, especially late in the game when the Appalachians still lie ahead.

My overall average speed at the arrival of TS 44 was 9.85 mph, and I still had 400 difficult miles of the toughest climbs of RAAM in front of me.

I asked Joe to start a spreadsheet so that he and the other navigators could document my progress. The spreadsheet would include an hour by hour account, from here on to the finish, of my miles traveled, miles left, average mph, remaining hours and required average mph to complete RAAM. Everyone including myself was to be kept informed at all times of my status.

We pulled out of Athens at about 9:00 a.m. RAAM and local time and Rudy, from KDLK in Del Rio, called for his daily morning interview. Joni talked with him and explained to the listeners that I was on the time bubble. She asked all the listeners in Del Rio to send as much spirit as possible to push me across these last 400 miles.

As we crossed the Ohio River, Joe yelled out over the PA system, "Ohio, DONE! Welcome to Parkersburg, West Virginia!"

Heading to TS45, the RAAM route book warned the racers: "The most difficult climbing in RAAM now begins. The altitude doesn't approach that of the Rocky Mountains, but the climbs are relentless. There is more elevation gained in this section than between any other consecutive time stations anywhere from coast to coast. In fact this and the next two sections are the three with the most climbing. But the most difficult measured in feet of climbing per mile ridden is still ahead between Cumberland and Hancock all in the mountains of . . . . Maryland!"

Right after Parkersburg I had two steep 150-foot climbs. There were many 250-foot climbs within the next 20 miles. My legs were screaming, but I needed to push; I had to get my mph back up. My goal now was to make that spreadsheet Joe was keeping look better and faster with each passing hour. I was no longer racing across America or from time station to time station. I was now racing hour to hour.

Team Dex arrived TS45. Ellenboro, WV. 2609 miles. 264 RAAM hours.

CJG: "Quote o' the day and of the hour: 'When God wants to do something wonderful, it begins with a difficulty. And if he wants to do something extremely wonderful, it begins with an impossibility.' From Charles B. Woehrle, age 94, P.O.W. The wonderfulness is now yours for the taking, Dex. You are not your body. May you start now the great race you wanted to end last year. 100 miles, three rides each, and then a cool-down ride, jaunts you have done dozens AND DOZENS of times. The hills will be good to you: one mile at a time. Rooting for Dex-n-motion from Montreal, Montana and Boise, Idaho."

The McCunes: "As Jackson Browne says, 'Whatever it is you might think you have nothing to lose . . . Through every dead and living thing time runs like a fuse . . . And the fuse is burning . . . And the earth is turning . . . Though the years give way to uncertainty . . . And the fear of living for nothing strangles the will . . . There's a part of me that speaks to the heart of me . . . Though sometimes it's hard to see . . . It's never far from me . . . Alive in eternity . . . That nothing can kill.' Nothing can kill the dream you have hatched, and that we have adopted. My name is Don, and I am a Dexaholic. Godspeed my friend!"

Brenda: "Dex I went to the movies today and all I could think about was you and Joni. You'll have missed so many good movies these past several days. Can't wait for you to get back as hometown heroes. You are greatly missed at spin class. We love you Dex!!!!!!"

Sandy: "Hills !!! OMG !!! I don't know how you do it coming from the 'flat lands'!!! Especially cruel put near the end of such a ride! Think 'carrot' . . . you're almost there!!!! Whoo Hoo !!!!!!"

Chapter 12

BEWARE THE APPALACHIANS

For RAAM racers, the Appalachian Mountains are shrouded in an aura of intimidation, if not of fear. RAAM has been called a race of truth, a race where an individual travels to the extremes of both their physical and mental limits. Call it a vision quest if you will. When asked why they race RAAM, some riders will tell you it is because they want to discover who they really are deep inside; they want to push themselves to that ultimate realm where they are introduced to an inner self they have never before met. Well, the Appalachians will grant them their wish and the racer better be prepared for who he or she meets.

The Appalachians are 150-plus miles of what seems like endless repetitive climbs that are much steeper than the climbs in the Rockies and longer than the climbs in the Ozarks. Couple that with the fact that you have already been racing for over 2500 miles when you encounter them and you can understand what makes the Appalachians so daunting.

Drivers in the follow vehicles must be alert at all times as the roads are narrow and usually without shoulders. The racer must be careful to avoid land mine-like potholes that can take a bike and racer down in an instant. The climbs are steep and winding with many blind curves. In 2010, while driving Shadow, Joni actually dozed off on one of the narrow, snaky climbs around Grafton, West Virginia and a guardrail was the only thing that kept her from driving off a cliff. Racers will see a road sign that reads, "8% grade next 5 miles" and they will struggle and work to get through those five difficult miles only to crest the climb and see yet another sign that reads, "8% grade next 5 miles."

There is also a historical mystique about the Appalachians, acquired over the years of RAAM races, which every rider must face. In 2004, Jure Robic became so delusional and his hallucinations so severe near Keyser, West Virginia that he actually thought he was in a combat situation and being fired upon. He hallucinated that the roadside mailboxes were his enemy. He got off his bike and physically attacked one of the mailboxes, uprooting it from the ground. In 2005, Jure became so paranoid and disoriented in the Appalachians that he accused his crew of driving him in circles. He stopped at a country store and, even though he was in first place by hours, refused to go on. He distrusted his crew and said he was through with them and with RAAM. It was only after lengthy persuasion by his crew chief, Matjaz Paninsek, he got on his bike and completed his RAAM victory.

Another example was the experience of Gerhard Gulewicz, an Austrian and top RAAM contender. He finished second behind Jure in 2009 and 2010 and was racing his sixth RAAM in 2011. Amy McFaddin had related to me back in Oxford, Ohio that she had talked with Gerhard and he had informed her that he was withdrawing at Grafton, West Virginia. He told her he just couldn't face the Appalachians one more time. Gerhard was in third place overall when he withdrew.

I knew I was behind the eight ball of time when I departed Ellenboro. I also knew my average miles per hour would be dropping significantly in the difficult Appalachians ahead. As the saying goes: welcome to the suck!

Conice and crew were due up for rotation in Shadow, but Joni decided to substitute Em for Michael as driver. Because of the time bubble, it was her strategy to give Michael a break so she could utilize him for a long, final push into Annapolis.

We were in Greenwood, West Virginia—another one of those "Green" towns—when we came upon a serious car accident right in front of us at an approaching intersection. Emergency vehicles of all types had responded to the scene. There were injuries in the accident and the city police had halted all traffic while EMS personnel extricated the patients from the wreckage. It was obvious that this was going to take some time.

I took the opportunity to get off my bike and sit in the navigator's seat in Shadow. Anika offered me a Balance Bar and Emergen C while she massaged my shoulders and Conice and Em busied themselves looking at the route book and searching on their phones for a possible alternate route. Conice eventually called the RAAM War Room to discuss the situation and the officials there were quick to find an approved detour to bypass the accident. As per RAAM protocol, Conice was given specific instructions on how we could proceed legally and without penalty.

The detour rerouted us slightly and picked back up immediately on the other side of the accident. By the time I was back on the RAAM route, though, I had lost another 30 precious minutes.

As I continued through the hills of West Virginia, I found myself having more and more difficulty shifting my gears. I thought it was a mechanical problem with my shifters and I kept cussing Dan under my breath. However, it slowly began to dawn on me that the real culprit was nerve damage in my hands. I normally climb with my hands resting on the drops of my handlebars because this gives me more strength to push up the mountains.

However, in 2010, my palms had become so bruised and traumatized from all the climbing, that I decided this year I would do most of my climbing with my hands on the hoods of my handlebars. This took most of the strain off my palms but at the expense of transferring the trauma from my palms to the webbing between my index fingers and thumbs. Many miles and hours of climbing while putting pressure on the webbing had caused nerve damage in both hands. The medial and radial nerves in my wrist were so damaged that I was losing function and strength in my thumbs and index fingers—precisely the fingers I needed to shift the gears efficiently. Although I didn't fully realize it at the time—I kept blaming a mechanical malfunction—I didn't have enough strength in my thumb to push the Campy shifter knob down when I needed a faster gear or push the shifter lever inside when I needed a climbing gear. In fact, all ten digits in both hands were completely numb.

It wouldn't be until well after RAAM, in September of 2011, I would find out from a hand surgeon that I had permanent muscle atrophy in the webbing between my thumbs and first fingers. Electronic nerve and muscle tests revealed significant damage that would take months to recover if, in fact, I would recover at all.

It is amazing the simple everyday things for which we use our thumbs—everyday actions we simply take for granted. For example, even as I write, months after RAAM 2011, I still have no sensation in the tips of my fingers and when I smear shave cream on my face I do well not to get it in my eyes or in my ears. Buttoning a shirt is totally impossible; there is no way I am able to push that little white round object through that elliptical slit. And thank goodness for Velcro on shorts—post-RAAM I went on a business trip and Joni had to alter my Dockers with Velcro just so I could fasten them! Then there was the time I went to a party where I was the honorary guest and I was totally embarrassed when I locked myself in the restroom because I didn't have enough strength in my thumb to unlock the little knob on the stall door. And how about the time I stopped at a convenience store to fill up with gas and had to ask a nearby girl to remove my gas cap. Now I know how my dog Koko feels without having thumbs!

But you don't stop racing RAAM just because you don't have thumbs—and the climbing continued. There were several 200-foot and 300-foot crests over the next few miles and I just kept standing and pushing with all the strength I could muster. As nightfall came, Conice navigated me through the thick traffic in Clarksburg at the US 50 freeway interchange. I rode through Bridgeport, Belgium, Prunytown and Fetterman in a mental daze, not really paying attention to anything except trying to maintain my relentless forward motion . . . RFM!

Team Dex arrived TS46. Grafton, WV. 2674 miles. 272 RAAM hours.

It was just before midnight when I pulled out of Grafton and headed toward Keyser. I knew from my memory of 2010 that the next 70 miles would be some of the hardest, sustained climbing I had yet to face. I also knew, because of the ticking RAAM clock, that I could not afford to lose any more time. The treacherous two-lane road with its long steep climbs would test me like I had never been tested in my life. The next 70 miles would very well be the deciding factor between becoming an elite member of the small family of RAAM solo finishers or just another RAAM DNFer.

The thought of not finishing again this year terrorized me and Michael Tarbet's words echoed through my mind. When I had publicly announced my return to RAAM 2011 to take care of unfinished business, everyone backed me and told me how they knew I would make it this time. Everyone instilled confidence in me by telling me how close Team Dex had come in 2010—even as rookies—and how 2011 would be different, given our experience with the race. They urged me on by telling me how great a job I had done in 2010 even with some of the worst weather in RAAM history. Everyone told me I had it in the bag in 2011—that is, every one except Michael.

Michael had warned me, "What if your effort in 2010 was the very best you could ever do? What if your 2010 was the ride of a lifetime? You think you had a hard time psychologically and emotionally handling defeat in 2010, just imagine how much of an impact it is going to be on you if you fail in 2011."

He warned me about going back to RAAM for all the wrong reasons, like guilt, revenge and regret. He told me to only go back because I loved it, because the odds were that I would not finish. He explained how there are so many other factors that must come together to complete RAAM other than just riding—finances, vehicle reliability, medicine, food, health, weather, crew mentality and support, roadways, etc. He said, "It's just amazing to me given all the variables how anyone can complete the race. You can be strong and determined, but it all has to come together. The odds are against you."

Now here I was on the dark roads in the Appalachian Mountains facing the reality of Michael's words. The temperature was in the low 60s as raindrops began to fall, obstructing my vision. As I started a 1.5 mile 6% climb I stood on my pedals and I attacked. This was no time to be lax. I couldn't afford to go out too hard and blow up, but at the same time I had to be aggressive or I would lose too much time.

There was a half mile 9% descent after the crest of Thornton Hill on a narrow road with no shoulder. I tried to stay in the middle of the road as much as possible because leaves and tree branches lined the edge. The twisty route made it difficult for Damaris to keep me in her headlight beams, especially on the hairpin turns. I was surprised my descending phobia did not overwhelm me as I dropped down the grade. Certainly I was cautious on the wet roads but I did better than I normally do on the downhills.

After the descent, it was flat for eight or nine miles before I started a five mile 6% climb. I screamed, "Ahhhhhhhh! Ahhhhhhh!" as I stood on my pedals and climbed even though I knew Dan and crew could hear me through the headset and I thought about how ridiculous I must sound to them. My quads were screaming. My heart felt like it was at the top of my throat. It just kept pounding and pounding. I felt like at any moment I was going to regurgitate my heart in one big heave. I would stand, climb and scream for as long as I could before the lactic acid would build up in my legs and my lungs to a point that I could no longer maintain, and then I would back off and recover. I repeated this sequence over and over again.

I crested the Friends Gap climb and began a 9% descent with three sharp hairpin turns. By now the temperature had dropped into the mid 50s. It was close to 3:00 a.m. and I was once again weaving from exhaustion. My leggings, bib shorts and jersey were soaking wet, more from my sweat than the raindrops. I was burning up as I climbed the mountains but I was freezing on the descents.

Finally, I told Dan I had to go down for a sleep. I found a wide spot in the road to pull over and Elaine helped me remove my wet gear and dried me off with a towel. She dressed me with dry undershirt, jersey and bibs, then I crawled up into my space and I was out.

Elaine woke me after a little less than two hours. I had no concept of time. I could have slept for five minutes or five hours and I would not have been able to tell the difference. She forced me to drink a flask of Ensure and some Vitamin water, and take a bite of a Cliff Bar. Then while totally disoriented as to time and place, I got back on my bike.

I crossed Wolf Creek and began a three mile 8% climb. I again screamed with my effort up the hill. The road leveled off just for a short distance as I temporarily crossed into Maryland where US 50 became the George Washington Highway, then the road climbed once more and, within 10 miles, I crossed the North Branch of the Potomac River and I was back in West Virginia.

To me, the small West Virginia communities resembled the ghost towns of west Texas as I passed through them in the wee hours of the night—Gormania, Hartmansville and Skyline. I climbed Difficult Hill, Mt. Storm, Allegheny Mountain and crossed Cheat River, Difficult Creek, and Abrams Creek. It was eerie at times as the names of the small towns and creeks brought forth memories of dueling banjos and the film *Deliverance*.

Damaris was doing the best she could under the circumstances to keep me in her headlights. I continued through the night screaming up the hills and giving it everything I had. This was no time for Dan's soft voice and Rik Fritz stories. He didn't even have time to read Facebook comments. Dan was totally concentrated on navigating and keeping me informed of the terrain that lay ahead. The night finally gave way to the light of dawn and I welcomed the morning sun as it peeked through the early morning fog. At least I could see the potholes and debris on the road now—it was amazing I hadn't crashed somewhere during the dark of the night.

Dan informed me that I was about 10 miles out of Keyser and most of the difficult climbing was behind me and that I had a 5 mile 9% descent coming up. My clothing was once again wet, so I decided to stop in Hartmansville to put dry gear on for the cold descent. Before we got there, in order to lose as little time as possible during the change, I asked Elaine to prepare a dry jersey, bibs, jacket, gloves, liners and the head warmer I would need. I also told her to be sure and have a towel ready for me to dry off with before I put on the dry clothes.

I rode into Keyser 9.5 hours after leaving Grafton which meant that, including my sleep and stops to change clothes, I had averaged less than 8 mph. I thought to myself, *What happened to that magic number 10? How in the world am I going to make up the lost time? Dang, I still have more of the Appalachians in Maryland coming up!*

The very sobering fact was that I arrived at the time station in Keyser at 9:04 a.m., after racing over 2700 miles and for nearly 12 days, a mere 43 minutes faster than the minimum RAAM arrival time—I only had 43 minutes in the bank and nearly 250 miles still to go. The demons of 2010 were on my front step.

Team Dex arrived TS47. Keyser, WV. 2744 miles. 282 RAAM hours.

Stacy Tooke: "Went to sleep last night and got up praying for you Dex. What do you say to someone who's ridden over 2700 miles. You're Awesome—Stay Hard."

R. Rojas: "If you are prepared, you will be confident, and will do the job.—Tom Landry. Team Dex IS PREPARED and WILL get 'Unfinished Business' taken care of! Go Team Dex! Almost at the finish line!"

Emile Abbot: "We all continue to be so proud of your efforts and accomplishments, Dex. You have just completed one of the toughest parts. We know the battle continues but we believe you are the David against this Goliath. We know you will find the way to defeat this monster of

3000+ miles. Take any strength you need from your fans, the sirens of the sea are calling you to Annapolis. Ride hard, ride strong and ride proud, Dex. This is your moment, this is your time, this is your destiny. Good luck, my friend, our prayers and thoughts are with you all the way."

Adriana: "So very proud of you!!! 245 to go . . . God bless you, Dex!!! Much love to you and Team Dex. Today is the day!!!"

Dave Elsberry's crew: "Dex, thank you for the encouragement . . . we are in this together! Keep pushing . . . YOU CAN DO THIS! We all believe in you Dex and we will celebrate at the finish line!"

Chapter 13

PUTTING FLINTSTONE TO REST

We now had less than 26 hours to make it to Annapolis. We had entered a very intense and precarious phase of the race, so Joni decided there would be no more crew rotations all the way to the finish. She then chose who she felt were the three most critical crew members to accompany her in Shadow for the final push in to Annapolis—which meant there would be four in Shadow rather than the normal three-person crew compliment. Michael was chosen as driver because he had proven he could drive like the Energizer Bunny with little or no sleep—and he was our trusted MacGyver. Joni selected Joe as navigator because he was the one person on the entire crew who I would actually listen to over the PA or headset. Also, RAAM 2010 had psychologically done a number on Joe just like it had on Joni and she trusted he would do whatever it took to get me to that finish banner. Dan was selected because he was our number cruncher, bicycle mechanic, and his navigation skills surpassed Joe's, just in case. And even though Elaine was the better domestique, Joni chose herself because there was no way in hell she wasn't going to be there for the closing chapter.

Before I departed the time station in Keyser, Joe said, "Come over here Dex, I want to show you something." On his laptop, he then proceeded to run a video made by Eldon Brown, a great friend of mine from Del Rio and a key member of my 2010 RAAM crew. He had taken the video of himself on his daily training ride and I could hear the wind noise as I watched Eldon's video camera capture the view over his handlebars and the familiar Highway 90 in Del Rio.

In the video Eldon said, "I've been following you the whole way. You are doing good but it is getting down to the nut cutting, you're going to have to get with it. I'm going to get you on my wheel. I want you to imagine I'm out there with you. I want you to hop on my wheel and I'm going to take you in. I'm going to take you to that last 100 yards. I'm going to be your lead-out domestique then I'm going to pull off and you are going to sprint that last 100 yards to the finish. So you take care, man, and you hop on my wheel and let's go. I luv you man, see ya!"

Tears came to my eyes as I watched Eldon riding and heard his voice; it meant so much to me. I would definitely have him at my side as I made my way to Annapolis.

At only 28.5 miles, the route from TS47 to TS48 was one of the shortest in RAAM, but naturally it still had its share of climbs since we were still in the Appalachians. As we crossed the north branch of the Potomac River I started a one-mile climb and once again entered Maryland for the second of four times. The route also required a heads-up navigator as there were several key turns in the last ten miles. In fact, in 2010, we had gotten lost on this section and ended up on a freeway. Once we figured it out—that we were off-route—I had to be put in Shadow and driven back to the point where I had strayed off course. I certainly didn't want that to happen again this year—we didn't have the time to waste.

Then there were other memories of RAAM in 2010. That year, Bob Hilton, a friend from Pennsylvania, had driven to Cumberland to meet up with Team Dex. Bob, along with his wife and daughter, stood on the corner at the time station, and cheered me on with a huge painted tarp that read, "Go, Dex, Go!" I was in horrible condition and nearing my end at that point, though, and I could barely keep my bike upright. Mark Biggs, one of my crew members, had to hold my bike for me and lean it to one side a bit just so I could raise my leg high enough to swing it over the top tube and dismount. I hadn't bathed or shaved in 12 days, my face was sunburned, my skin looked like an old, worn football, and I had half-dollar sized water blisters on both forearms from so much time in the aerobars. The slits in the front of my helmet had caused predominant alternating sunburn marks on my forehead.

Eldon had been driving Shadow and went over to visit with Bob while I did my best Tim Conway impersonation and limped over to Bessie. After a short 15-minute power nap and an attempt at keeping an egg sandwich down, I exited Bessie. I mustered a short wave and forced smile to Bob and family as I climbed back on my bike and headed out of the time station. Eldon and Bob continued to converse as I took off and Bob commented,

"He looks terrible. I have never seen anyone in that condition in my entire life. How long has he been this way?"

Eldon replied, "He's been like this for about five or six days now."

Bob actually had a tear in his eye when he said, "When I saw him go into that RV, I didn't think he would ever come back out. I am fearful for him. I don't know how anyone can continue in his state."

"You don't understand." replied Eldon. "This is what these kinds of guys do. This is what they train and work for. This is what he strives for."

Team Dex arrived TS48. Cumberland, MD. 2772 miles. 284 RAAM hours.

This time, I spent only five minutes off my bike at TS48 in Cumberland before I was off and racing again. It was close to noon and I was immediately faced with one of the most challenging sections of the race. The RAAM route book says of this section: "The four major climbs in this section are tough. The last climb (up Sideling Hill) could be a walker. This is the most difficult section of RAAM, measured in feet of climbing per mile."

This section had a lot more significance to me than just being a difficult ride. It was here, at Flintstone, Maryland, that my RAAM ended in 2010. This year, though, I was a different rider. I was in much better condition at this point in the race and no way was I going to stop this time.

As I approached the small gas station where my race had ended in 2010, Bessie and crew were already there to greet me with signs of motivation and cheer. Anika was wearing a Jimmy Durante plastic nose and a cap while she held a sign aloft that said, "I gotta take a S#$&!" (One of my more common phrases.) Damaris had donned a brightly colored Afro wig and orange glasses and her sign said, "Go, Princess, Go!" Conice had a sign that read, "Gosh dang it!" Elaine was wearing a T-shirt with two huge red bull's-eye targets strategically positioned over her chest and her sign said, "This ain't last year!" Finally, Em was wearing a toy six-shooter and held a sign that read, "Don't Mess With Dex!"

Inside Shadow, Joe and crew took turns on the PA system with cheers and congratulations. I looked one more time at Elaine's sign and thought to myself, *This sure as hell ISN'T last year. I gotta do this!*

Immediately after Flintstone, I started the climb up Polish Mountain, the first of the four hard climbs, with a constant 8% to 9% grade. I was moving uphill at barely 6 mph. It was then that Joe decided he would use my slow pace as an opportunity to take some photos from ahead of me instead of the thousands he had taken from behind my butt. He got out of Shadow and began running up the hill so he could position himself for the shot when I came by. I let him run for a little bit, then just when he thought he was far enough ahead of me to take the photo, I gave a push and sprinted right up next to him before he could shoot. This forced him to run further up the hill—and again I waited for the right moment, then pushed hard and passed him before he could take his photo. Michael, Dan and Joni were laughing and telling me to take it easy on him. Joe finally did get a couple of good face shots of me as I climbed, and the whole episode kept us all entertained.

The toughest of the four climbs leading into Hancock was Sideling Hill at over three miles in length and a continuous 8% grade, with short spurts of over 10%. On this one, my quads were soon screaming and I was zigzagging across the pavement to keep from having to walk up the hill, barely moving at five mph. If I had gone any slower, I would have fallen off of my bike. To change muscles, I would stand for 8 or 10 pedal revolutions then I would sit on my saddle for 8 or 10 revolutions; I kept alternating back and forth. I focused on my breathing, making sure I was taking in as much air as possible into my lungs. I relaxed my shoulders and hands. I was determined to send all that oxygenated blood to my legs and not waste any of it on my arms or hands. I made sure I was using my quads, the biggest muscle in my body to propel me up the hill.

To help get me to the top of Sideling, Michael played one of my best 5 O'clock Rocker climbing songs, *Tour de France* from the *Breakin'* soundtrack. The song gets its inspiration from the famous stage of the Tour de France which climbs Alpe d'Huez. It starts out with no music—just the rhythmic heavy breathing of a rider as he is working his way up the mountain—then the song slowly introduces a rhythmic drum beat that sounds like the beating of a hard-working heart. It is a good seven minutes in length and I would typically use it in spin class as my final song of the day. I would tell everyone to crank the resistance up on their bikes and stand with me as we climbed. I would push them into a final crescendo of heavy breathing as we vicariously made our way up Alpe d'Huez. Now I was using that same song to get me up Sideling Hill, but this time it wasn't a vicarious experience—it was real life. And oh my, did it hurt!

I finally crested Sideling Hill then, instead of being able to recover and let my muscles rest on the descent, I was once again tense and braking as I slowly went down the other side.

Joe and Dan continued keeping track of my hourly miles traveled and comparing them to the number of remaining hours and miles. I was right on the bubble. I worried, *How can I average 10 mph when I'm spending all day riding five mph up hills? What if we have another detour or more construction or another traffic accident or anything that could delay me even more!*

Team Dex arrived TS49. Hancock, MD. 2809 miles. 289 RAAM hours.

I rolled through the Hancock, Maryland TS without stopping and Joe called my arrival time in to the War Room and received his confirmation number. Then, I hadn't gone but a mile when I saw a road sign: "Welcome to Pennsylvania." Not far after that, as sort of a cruel welcome gift perhaps, I rounded a curve and couldn't believe what I saw: a 300-foot climb of at least 13% grade. I stopped to take a pee before I started the climb but, when I tried to restart, the hill was too steep and I couldn't get clipped into my pedals without falling over. Dan got out of Shadow and walked with me as I pushed my bike up the climb. *Gosh dang it! I thought the four hills leading into Hancock spelled the last of the climbing! Nobody said anything about this monster! This is way tougher than Sideling! Why isn't it mentioned in the route book?* Eventually, the grade lessened and I was back in the saddle.

The route kept taking us back and forth through Maryland and Pennsylvania; one minute I was in one state, and the next minute in the other.

About eight miles later I came to a 'Y' intersection and I saw a man with a woman and kids standing beside the road with "Go, Team Dex!" signs. It turned out to be my nephew Chris Walls and his family. Chris lives in Maryland and had helped support me in 2010, now here he was again cheering me on. The encounter gave me a really wonderful moral boost.

Then, naturally, came yet another climb, a sustained five-mile uphill section with the last 1.5 miles at an 8% grade. I will tell any future RAAM racer right here and now, do not believe the RAAM route book when they tell you, "This is the last climb in RAAM." They are cruel liars! There is always another climb in RAAM!

As we neared Greencastle, Pennsylvania—yeah, that's right, another "Green" town—Joe got on the headset to tell me we had a detour coming up. "A detour?" I groaned. "You have to be kidding me. How long is the detour? How much further will I have to ride? How long will it take me? How much more time will I lose?" I rattled off the questions in quick succession in total frustration.

Joe patiently replied, "Earlier today there was a festival in Greencastle which closed down traffic to the main street. The festival isn't going on now, but other RAAM racers that came through at that time had to take a detour around the town. Therefore, to maintain the integrity of RAAM, all racers are being required to take the same detour." I couldn't believe it. Here I was, on the time bubble, and I had to detour around a town because of a road closure that was no longer in effect. Thankfully, we were able to navigate through the required routing on side streets and back to the published RAAM route with minimal time loss.

The next "fun" incident occurred near Waynesboro, Pennsylvania on a two-lane road with a narrow shoulder and, of course, congested traffic. Despite the other cars trying to pass us, a local cyclist pulled up beside me and started talking to me like I was his new BFF. He was making me very nervous riding so close in the midst of the heavy traffic. My coordination and riding skills at this point were nonexistent and this guy was riding inches away from me while shooting video with his camera. It was difficult to hear what he was saying over the traffic noise, but apparently he was a local cyclist from Waynesboro and he had been greeting and videoing each RAAM racer as they passed through the town. I explained to him that was very cool but right now I needed him to back off; I didn't want his company. He ignored what I said and kept riding even closer to me.

In Shadow, Joe could see what was taking place and was getting just as nervous as I was. He got on the PA system and kindly asked the guy to back off, but still the guy stayed right with me. He was starting to be a total nuisance to Joe and me, so Joe got back on the PA and sternly said, "Get away from Dex. Do not ride with him anymore."

The guy kept riding beside me and made some excuse like, "It's only a couple more miles until the road widens and it will all be okay."

I got totally pissed off and said, "Look buddy, I don't care how far it is, get the hell away from me." And then, just like a little puppy you can't get rid of, he extended his arm for a handshake and says, "Okay, just give me a little love!"

I just looked over at the guy and said, "Seriously? Just go away!"

He finally pulled off at a Dairy Queen and, as Shadow went by, Joe and crew gave him the evil eye. The guy looked as if he were going to wait at the DQ to ambush and pester the next RAAM rider who came through. I don't think he had any understanding at all of what RAAM does to a rider after nearly 3000 miles in the saddle.

Team Dex arrived TS50. Rouzerville, PA. 2858 miles. 295 RAAM hours.

Rik Fritz, from Flagstaff: "We are all pulling for you, Dex, you can do this. Dig deep buddy and keep those wheels rolling. You are so close now, keep going. When you cross that finish line, that cheer you hear will be all of us across this country who have been rooting for you. Keep it up Dex, you've got this!"

Jason G: "Give 'em hell, Dex. Nothing worth doing is easy. I'm with you in spirit, but I'm going to bed. Cowboy up. God bless and be safe."

James: "Dex . . . you are so close. Along with many other RAAM fans, I've been pulling for you all week as I've been keeping track of the riders—a friend raced as part of a relay team. You ARE going to make it . . . keep riding, brother, you are an inspiration to so many of us, young, old, and everything in between."

Dalia Blanco: "Burning the midnight oil with you, you're not alone. Feel the energy. So speed ahead and get it done, we all need some sleep. :)"

Rae Connor: "Now you just need to do your normal weekend ride, but this time there will be a RAAM 2011 Finish Line at the end!"

Belinda Reyes: "Smell the salt water . . . feel the ocean breeze . . . think about seafood & Dr. Pepper . . . It's right there . . . & we can ALL feel it with you! Song dedication for Dex & his amazing spirit: *Not Every Man Lives* by Jason Aldean. Enjoy your moment!!!"

Chapter 14

TRYING TO FIND IT

I arrived at TS50 on June 26th at 9:33 p.m. RAAM time. The minimum RAAM cut-off time at that check point was 10:00 p.m. so I had only 27 minutes in the bank with over 130 miles to go. Every muscle in my body was aching as my body continued to deteriorate. My face was scarred from the sun, I was wearing double cycling gloves hoping to keep the nerve damage in my hands from getting worse, both elbows had bandages to help pad the tender skin, and both knees were criss-crossed with Rock Tape. I looked like a wounded soldier in battle, which I guess is exactly what I was.

My saddle sores were nothing short of open-skinned wounds now. Both feet were burning from a cycling injury known as "hot foot", a burning pain in the ball of my foot that was radiating toward the toes. My feet felt like some sadistic demon was applying a blow torch.

I sure could have used a good massage, too. I realize you have to play the lottery to win, but if I ever do play and win the lottery, the first thing I will do is hire Lance's masseuses and bike mechanics as live-ins. I would get a massage and I would have my bike washed and tuned daily.

The only thing worse than my current physical condition was my mental state. The 12 days of extreme physical exertion coupled with the long hours of sleep deprivation were playing a head game on me. I was losing focus.

When you combined these worsened physical and mental states together it equaled slower speed. At a time when I could not afford it, I was getting slower and slower. Joe and Dan continued to crunch the numbers on the spreadsheet and my average mph was dropping below the red line. At the rate I was going now, I would not add my name to that elusive RAAM-finisher role call.

Unfinished Business

As the crew continued to crunch the numbers, the nightmare of 2010 began to haunt Joe. While Joe wasn't a cyclist, RAAM 2010 had given him a tremendous sense of awe and respect for me and my chosen sport. He watched me dig down deep time and time again as I would somehow find the energy to get back on that bike or climb another mountain. Joe had wanted that finish line very badly in 2010. He wanted it mostly for me, partly for himself, and partly for the crew along with all the Dexans. It had been my dream and he so badly wanted me to have it to cherish forever.

Joe knew more about the throngs of supporters following me on my website than I did. He had looked forward to writing that final report and sharing with them the happy ending to my amazing adventure that they all so desperately wanted. As an athlete himself, it had been embedded in him to keep pushing for the prize.

As the race progressed, though, and the battle against the clock and finish line had intensified, Joe had something else pressuring him. Much more so than me, Joe had always been the athlete in the family. He excelled in tennis and for years he was one of the top ranked master tennis players in Texas. Unfortunately, Joe's famed tennis career was haunted by several "almost" tournaments—just like the sport's cliché of "never winning the big one", Joe was plagued with a series of "almost" titles. He was all too familiar with being so close to the big prize and falling just short. So, in 2010, when I withdrew from RAAM, it became another "almost" for Joe.

When Team Dex dropped out of RAAM in Flintstone, Maryland, he had crawled into the loft in Bessie, pulled his sunshades down over his eyes so no one else could see, buried his face in a pillow and wept most of the way to Annapolis. In his demented state, he felt as though he had let me down. Now, in 2011, Joe was getting very close to another "almost."

It was after midnight when I traveled through Gettysburg National Historic Park. It was quite eerie seeing the headstones of the fallen soldiers on both sides of the road as I passed by. My mind started playing tricks on me and it was difficult to distinguish shadows from actual objects. I guess I wasn't accustomed to seeing Civil War cannons on the side of the road.

Team Dex arrived TS51. Hanover, PA. 2898 miles. 299 RAAM hours.

I was desperate for sleep. Following in Shadow, Dan and Joe noticed that every so often I made a jerking motion with my head while at the same time I would weave as if to correct my line of travel. Dan made the comment, "He must be nodding off again."

Michael replied, "That isn't when he is nodding off. That's when he is waking up!"

Then, all of a sudden, I braked and came to a complete stop on the dark, deserted highway.

Joe asked through the headset, "What are you doing?"

"That truckload of potatoes pulled right out in front of me!"

Joe turned to Michael, "Oh boy, he's hallucinating again."

It was close to 3:00 a.m. and it had been 24 hours since my last sleep in Macomber, West Virginia. My speed continued to drop. Luckily the traffic was light because I was weaving drastically from one side of the traffic lane to the other. Joe kept talking to me, trying to keep me awake but, even so, he caught me twice actually weaving across the center stripe of the roadway. He yelled loudly into the headset, "Dex, you come across that centerline one more time and I am pulling you off that bike! Your RAAM will be over. I am dead serious!"

Joni, as crew chief, had a critical decision to make. Should she put me down for a sleep, or let me ride? She couldn't put me down for more than 15 minutes or so because the entire RAAM could be lost for sure—we had very little time to spare. If she let me keep riding, my current pace was so slow that I probably wouldn't make the cut-off anyway. She finally decided to put me down for a 15-minute power nap with the hope that I would wake up and my speed would increase.

I was nearing Manchester, Maryland when Joe told me to find a wide spot in the road. I pulled over and stopped, but Dan had to hold my bike for me because I couldn't even unclip from my pedals. Joni helped me with my helmet but I left my shoes on as I climbed up into my little cubby hole. I was comatose in no time.

Time was so critical that Joni timed my 15-minute sleep to the second. I awoke and immediately started asking questions. Joni just told me, "Shut up, we don't have time for your questions. You just need to get on your bike and ride!"

It was a little after 3:00 a.m. when I climbed back into the saddle—in less than nine hours the RAAM officials would turn off the clock at the finish line.

I began to ride again, but my speed did not improve. Joe and Dan looked at their charts and they could see that my average mph was continuing to drop below the critical line. At this point, Joe was desperate to do whatever he could to keep my RAAM from going down the tubes, so he grabbed the PA system mike, knowing I could hear him better than when he used the headset, and he started working on me.

"Dex, you gotta go faster. You have to push. Dex, what do you want to say in three weeks? Do you want to go back to Del Rio and tell all the Dexans that you did the best you could but just came up short?"

"When you get back are you going to accept a pat on the back and a congratulatory 'You did a great job even thought you didn't make it? Even worse, do you want to hear the words 'Better luck next year'!"

"When you get back to Del Rio and speak at the Lion's Club and the Rotary Club, how is your speech going to end, Dex? Are you going to tell them you didn't finish RAAM? Are you going to give them excuses?"

"Dex, you are writing that speech right now. You are writing your final chapter in RAAM. How is that chapter going to end, Dex? I want you to show me right now with your pedals and your body how that speech is going to end. Do it right now, Dex."

In a speech he gave at a post-RAAM party at the Bank and Trust in Del Rio, Joe would later describe my reaction to his words this way: "What I saw, I still get chill bumps thinking about, because the man took off. I mean, whoosh, he stood up on those pedals and took off. And we were all like, 'Oh, my gosh!' I just kept pushing him and driving him and he kept riding and riding and his mph average kept going up, up, up! What he did that night on that bicycle, under those circumstances, was one of the most incredible sights I have ever witnessed!"

Tears of joy poured from Joni as she saw me wake up. She said, "Guys, he is doing what he does best now. I've seen this before. He is going to make it!"

Michael commented, "Joe, I don't know exactly what you did, but keep it up!"

Dan called it the single most impressive demonstration of pure will he had ever seen.

I remained on my aero bars staring straight ahead. The only thing I could see in the dark of the night was Shadow's headlight beams. I thought about what Joe had said. I never wanted anything so badly in my entire life. I was more determined than ever to get this done, but I knew something had to change. I knew I had to somehow pick up my speed.

I pushed aside the burning pain of the saddle sores and ignored the loss of function in my nerve damaged hands. I refused to accept the delirium and exhaustion; all my ailments were of no consequence at this point. From now on, I would focus on only one thing and that was pedaling my ass to Annapolis!

Joe continued talking to me through the headset, pushing and driving me forward. He reminded me about the great time we had when I had run the Boston Marathon—he had traveled with Joni and me to Boston. The night before the Marathon, Joe had presented me with an inspirational poem, *Beacons of Light*, he had written for the occasion. In one key line, Joe had written, "Some men are content to sit on the bridge of time and wait for chance to surprise them with a special day. Others burn with a fiery desire to experience more than fate brings."

I thought about those words and said to myself, *Tonight, I'm not waiting for some storybook serendipity ending. I'm making my own fate right now!* I fought off my exhaustion and dug deep, and my average mph gradually started to improve.

One of my favorite sport's motivational speeches is from the movie, *The Miracle*, where Coach Brooks addresses the inexperienced players of the 1980 U.S. Olympic Hockey Team who are the huge underdogs facing off against the more mature and tremendously talented professional Soviet Team. Brooks tells his young players, "Great moments are born from great opportunity." He went on to tell them that they had earned their opportunity. Brooks said, "If we played them ten times, they might win nine, but not this game. Not tonight."

I drew on that speech for strength and motivation. I had earned my opportunity in RAAM with over 30 dedicated years of training. I had earned my spot in this race through sheer determination by logging 18,000 to 20,000 miles a year on my bike. I had qualified for this race at the Tejas 500 and now it was my turn and my moment. Considering the number of miles I had remaining and the deteriorated physical and mental state I was in, the odds were definitely against me just like they were against the United States Hockey team. However, I was not going to let it pass without giving it everything I had left. This was my moment and I was determined to make my final chapter in RAAM a successful one.

RAAM isn't just a bicycle race; it is a testing ground for life. It is a measure of one's own importance and values. I thought about how lucky I was to be raised the way I was by my Mom and Dad in a small town in West Texas. I recalled vivid memories of my high school days in Crane where no student went through the school system without learning about pride and determination. Now, 40 years later, I found I was still drawing on those values.

There is a dark side to RAAM, though; a side that only those who have been there know exists. In my experience, that dark side manifests itself in the form of nightmares. For months following RAAM in 2010, I continually found myself having the same seemingly endless nightmare of desperately racing from time station to time station only to find out that I never made it to the final one. I would awaken in the middle of the night with my sheets drenched from my cold sweat.

That year, following RAAM, I had withdrawn into a cocoon of solitude and depression. I wouldn't socialize with other riders and would only train by myself. As I faced the final miles in 2011, I was more determined than ever to rid myself of those nightmares and demons.

In 2010, Joe had presented me with a letter he had written the night before RAAM started. He wrote:

"Dex,

> Life is about choices, and the decisions that define men are often made in the midst of their toughest conflicts. You have chosen this starting line and the conflict awaiting. I can only make an attempt to find words to know, to explain, and understand this choice and the destination you seek. Whatever it is you are trying to find on this journey, may you find it more brilliant, more fulfilling, and more meaningful than you have imagined.

> Trying to Find It

> With great courage you push your front tire slowly to the start line. On the other side lies your dream and the monster who

seeks to crush you. The shear enormity and power of your foe is immense. At this moment, you dare not allow your eyes to view or your mind to consider him. Many battles lie ahead, and the strategy of your opponent is no secret. The first attack will be physical as arrows of pain and fatigue rain upon your body. As the physical battle intensifies, the mental conflict begins. The warrior inside you will fight with great pride and determination, but this foe is strong beyond words. With your body repeating, 'there is nothing left', and your mind delusional, doubt creeps in. In this critical moment, your foe will employ his ultimate strategy of victory, creating a war so violent, so full of destruction; he is no longer the opposition. The decisive battle will take place deep within, and the opponent will be yourself. This inner war culminates in a moment when time matters not and everything superficial in the world is stripped away. Only you, your bicycle, and the pure essence of what fuels your dream remain. Here you will find it. In this moment you might just realize the dream never really was about the finish line of RAAM, but is truly about a personal journey to a path of inner discovery, victory, and peace ending in a higher more meaningful life—for to conquer oneself is perhaps the greatest victory."

I thought about Joe's words. I thought about this violent war I was in and I thought about conquering not only RAAM, but winning the more extreme challenge of conquering myself. I stood on my pedals, pushed my thumb down on the gear shifter with all the strength I could muster, grabbed two gears and took off like the crazy, idiotic, possessed, lunatic that everyone has always thought I was.

Dan called in to the War Room as we approached TS52 in Mt. Airy, home of the last RAAM penalty box. If I had any penalties for rule violations, I would have to wait the time out here. But, great news—Team Dex had a green light! No penalties!

Unfinished Business

Team Dex arrived TS52. Mt. Airy, MD. 2935 miles. 302 RAAM hours.

Adrian Billings: "Dex, you are an amazing athlete and person. I am so proud of you!!!! Remember, relentless forward motion. I have always admired your dogged determination and you continue to amaze me. Ride on brother!!"

Pam Bunch: "You certainly have been flying like the Eagle you are, now is the time to dive. Let 'er go, Dex, you are there. So close, so close, I bet you can smell it!!!!!!!!!! So very proud of you and your team. I've seen you on the highway all tucked down in that dive bomb stance, now lets GO let 'er rip!!!! You can and will!"

Lauren and Merry Staffen: "The end is in sight! Way to go Dex and crew!"

Ray Hanselman: "Lance Armstong who?"

Roger Bollinger: "Dexter, this is Roger again. Its time to get mean, tear them pedals off of it. You have a heart like a bull and a head like a mule, get mean! You're the champion of the world as far as I'm concerned."

Lily Hernandez: "O M G!!!!!!!!! Where's my tissue box? I'm gonna need it!!! Make that two boxes . . . !"

Chapter 15

THE RAAM ROLL CALL

Bessie and crew were waiting for us at the Mt. Airy time station to cheer me on when I arrived. From here to the end, the RV would not be allowed on the course; they would have to take an alternate route. Joni reminded them, "You are on your own now. Bessie is not allowed at the dock in Annapolis, so take Bessie to the hotel and then find a taxi or shuttle to the finish line."

Conice's reply reflected the confidence and experience gained over the past 12 days: "You don't worry about us. We are RAAM grownups now and we can do anything!"

I had arrived at Mount Airy, Maryland at 5:42 am. With a RAAM minimum time cut-off of 6:15 a.m., I therefore had exactly 33 minutes in the bank with 54.6 miles to go. The sun was up and I was awake—I was riding well at precisely the moment when I so desperately needed to be doing so.

The road from Mount Airy to Odenton was described in the RAAM route book with the words "little traffic on rural roads for 25 miles, then congestion increases as the route crosses major arteries of the Washington to New York City northeast corridor."

All I can say is that the RAAM route book didn't take into consideration that a racer might be on that particular 25 miles of scenic rural road during the Monday morning rush of commuter traffic heading to the Annapolis metropolis. The road was a two-lane blacktop with little or no shoulder and there were miles of double-yellow stripes, that is, no-passing zones. It was extremely curvy—I'll bet there wasn't a straight half-mile on the entire route, and the Monday morning traffic was horrendous.

I thought the traffic in Missouri had been terrible, but Missouri was nothing compared to this stuff. Most of the time, there were streams of 40 to 50 irate, road-raged, motorists backed up behind us. There wasn't even enough shoulder or a wide spot sufficient for us to pull over to let them pass. In their desperation, they would pull around me with no regard for their own safety or the safety of oncoming traffic let alone the safety of the crazy idiot on the bike.

Drivers paid little or no attention to the no-passing zones. They were coming around Shadow and me on blind curves and uphill sections at top speeds. They would play chicken with oncoming traffic and duck in at the last moment to avoid a head-on collision.

Michael kept asking Joni, "Do I let people pass?"

Joni replied, "They can pass us, but you stay as close to him as you possibly can so they can't whip around us and reach him."

Michael stayed dangerously close to me. In his desire to protect my butt, he had those speakers on the front of Shadow within five feet of my rear wheel.

Dan chimed in with his observation, saying, "You know, throughout this entire race I have been considering doing RAAM as a relay team. But no way now—this is absolutely insane!"

Joni has had to put up with and witness my risk-taking lifestyle for nearly 40 years. Through my phases of exotic snakes, scuba diving and 14 years as a 911 paramedic on the streets, she has witnessed time and time again how I have put myself into dangerous situations. Throughout my cycling career she has learned to accept my passion to push myself to the extreme. Even before RAAM, she had seen me suffer several concussions from severe crashes, had patiently dealt with my frustration from bone fractures and had stood beside me for decades of endless training miles and races under the most extreme conditions.

Knowing how big RAAM was from our 2010 experience; Joni knew exactly the extremes I would have to go to in order to accomplish my dream. She had seen me face hypothermia, delirium, sleep deprivation, bodily injury, and even how I had to face my fear of descents. But now, as she sat in Shadow witnessing these horrific traffic conditions, she questioned it all. This was more terrifying than anything she had ever had to bear.

At this point Joni was so fearful for my life that she could hardly function. She started crying just to relieve the stress. She had already witnessed me get hit by a car once. She was horrified and could not bear the thought of seeing her husband's life flash before her eyes.

Joni told the crew in Shadow, "Guys, I can't be here. I can't watch this. This is too hard. I can't witness him get hit again."

As she cried, Dan put his hand on her shoulder and assured her, "Joni, he's going to be okay, he's going to be okay. We are going to take care of him."

Joni closed her eyes and prayed to herself, "God, just get us through this nightmare. Let us get this finished. Let us just be done with this."

As navigator and driver, respectively, Joe and Michael were focused intensely on what they were doing. There was really no talking or communicating among the crew other than the words necessary for supporting me and doing whatever they had to do for me.

We finally found a wide spot and pulled over. Michael went over to the bushes to take a leak while Dan and Joe just looked at each other in horror as the cars zoomed by. Joni had been riding in her cubbyhole in Shadow, witnessing the close calls as the cars passed. I saw her with her hands covering her face. She was trembling and crying uncontrollably.

I went over to her. In between sobs she told me how scared she was and how she feared for my life. She said, "RAAM isn't worth it. It is just a bicycle race. You are going to get killed out here!"

The sores in my mouth were so severe and my tongue so swollen that it was hard for me to speak, but I held her in my arms and said, "It's going to be okay, baby. I'll be alright. Michael has my back. I love you."

Joe told me, "Dex, we have to get back out there. We can't waste any more time."

The traffic was so steady that there wasn't even a break for us to cut in. Finally, Joni said, "Michael, let's all get ready to go. You just pull Shadow out into the traffic and block it so Dex can pull out."

Some minutes later, we finally made it out of that horrible section of rush-hour two-lane and eventually started working our way through a system of controlled-access highways. I never thought I would ever be so happy to be riding on a freeway in a metropolitan area, but I was so relieved to have multiple lanes and a wide shoulder, and not having to worry about oncoming cars. My biggest problems were negotiating the various exit and entrance ramps.

As the time ticked by, the only thing I could think about was that finish line. My speed picked up a bit more and I kept pushing. Even though I was still having trouble shifting my gears, I would grab two gears, stand and push hard for 30 or 40 second intervals, then sit down on my saddle and recover—then I would stand again for another interval, repeating this over and over again.

Michael did an incredible job of blocking traffic on the freeways. Joni was hanging out the window of Shadow, frantically waving her arms as she attempted to warn oncoming cars of my presence. Dan, in the very back of the van, was signaling Michael when it was okay for him to pull over as he approached the entrance ramps. Joe was constantly on the PA system letting me know when to go straight, when to pull to the right, when to pull to the left and when to just plain ole give it hell!

In the midst of all this chaos, Dexans around the country were going nutso. They were sitting on pins and needles trying desperately to obtain any available updates. They constantly clicked back and forth from the GPS tracker to the RAAM website to the ultradex website to the Dex Facebook fan page. They all knew it was going to be close.

Many comments were being left on Facebook: "How's his speed right now?" "I just woke up and I can't tell where he is." "I'm at work, is there going to be a live feed of the finish?" "Is KDLK going to have their morning interview?"

Joni received a phone call from Brian Argabright, sports editor of the Del Rio News Herald. She immediately told him she couldn't talk right now, "Things are just too intense!"

Being the persistent journalist he was, Brian threw in the quick question, "Off the record, is he going to make it?"

Joni snapped back, "If he doesn't get killed by a car!"

Team Dex arrived TS53. Odenton, MD. 2974 miles. 306.5 RAAM hours.

I was just a few miles from the finish when Joni received a call from Rudy at KDLK asking about the possibility of doing a live interview with her as I crossed the finish line, but she was too emotional at that point to talk with him. Joni assured him she would have Em give him a call when I arrived at the pier so the radio could cover it live.

About four miles from the Rams Head Roadhouse, we pulled over at a convenience store. By this time I had over an hour in the bank and Joni wanted me to look as nice as possible when I arrived at the pier, rather than looking like a war zone refugee. She insisted, "You are not wearing those ugly, stained, white shorts into the finish line!"

I stood behind the opened passenger door of the van to shield me from view as Joni and Michael helped me put on a fresh pair of dark bibs and my clean Race Across America Qualifier jersey. Michael helped me pull the double gloves away from my swollen fingers. The gloves were ragged and ripped. It had become a major struggle for me to remove the gloves, especially toward the end of the race when the nerve damage in my fingers had become so severe. I told Michael, "Throw those damn gloves away! I never want to see them again!"

Dan began to unwrap the extra padding off my handlebars and the extra cushion Joni had rigged on the elbow pads of my aero bars so that my bike would look like a normal racing bike rather than a Humvee fresh from a battlefield in Afghanistan. He also removed the headset microphone and speaker from my helmet.

Joni gave me some mouthwash to rinse with, hoping to give me some relief from the sores in my mouth and my swollen tongue. She then had me sit on the passenger seat sideways with my feet resting on the pavement as she ripped the strips of Rock Tape from my knees.

Team Dex arrived TS54. Annapolis MD. 2983 miles. 307 hours 20 min.

Most people think the finish of RAAM is at the finish banner at the Navy Pier, but there are actually three separate finish lines. The first one is TS54 at the Rams Head Roadhouse—this is the end of the timed portion of the race. However, at the Roadhouse, RAAM officials automatically add 26 minutes to every racer's elapsed time to cover the time it will take to get from there to the pier—this total becoming the official finish time. I mean, after all, you don't expect to be given anything in RAAM for nothing, do you?

The second finish is about two miles farther down the road from the Roadhouse at a Shell Gas station. Racers are met at this point by RAAM marshals and escorted, parade style, by an official RAAM vehicle over the last few miles to the crowds of people and media waiting at the third and final finish line, the City Dock.

For Team Dex, though, there was a fourth RAAM finish, and it was the most significant finish of them all. The fourth finish for me was between the Roadhouse and the Shell station. It was here that I actually realized I had finally caught the elusive dream I had so desperately been chasing. Joe put Joni's and my favorite RAAM theme song over the stereo speakers and Joni reached her hand out of the window of Shadow toward me. I carefully moved my bike closer to the van so I could touch hers as we both cried and listened to Matisyahu's, *One Day*. Joe was videoing this historic moment as he said, "Congratulations, brother, you did it. We love you."

Joni was in tears and crying as she cried, "You did it, baby!"

I was choking up myself as I told her, "I love you."

Joni replied, "I love you, too, sweetheart. We did it, baby. You did it! I am soooo proud of you!"

I was crying as I looked over at her and said, "It was a lot of hard work, baby."

"It was worth it." And she said again, "I am soooo proud of you! You are strong!"

Joe chimed in, "Incredible, brother!"

There wasn't a dry eye or clear throat in the van.

Joe yelled, "I love you, brother! Enjoy your ride! Enjoy your victory!"

My two favorite RAAM officials met me at the Shell station, Johnny Boswell and Jim Harms. They both congratulated me and the crew, and they allowed Joni to ride in the escort vehicle that would be parading me to the pier. I was riding at barely eight mph through the heavy traffic as Jim constantly kept honking his horn, not because of traffic congestion but because he was letting everyone know that a RAAM solo rider was completing the toughest bicycle race in the world. Cars honked back as people leaned out their windows to congratulate me. Pedestrians waved and cheered me on. The lead vehicle pulled off as I arrived at the finish chute.

Fans pushed forward, leaning on the temporary fencing cheering and clapping. It was like a crazy photo shoot. Everyone was taking photos and videos with cameras and cell phones so they could capture this special moment. I could hear George Thomas on the microphone as he announced my arrival to the crowd. On the other side of the banner, I could see the Bessie crew anxiously waiting to greet me as I crossed the elusive final finish line.

Being the awesome domestique she was, Anika was right there to help me dismount my bike. Then in RAAM tradition, with difficulty but determination, I stood under the Race Across America finish banner and raised my bike above my head in pride! My name could now be added to the elite RAAM role call.

The business was finished!

Team Dex arrived TS55. City Dock, Annapolis, MD. 2989.8 miles. 307 hours 46 minutes.

Doug Monroe: "Three weeks from now what are we going to say? I FINISHED RAAM!"

Brenda: "The journey is over!!!! I just saw your finish line video and you look so happy. Hope and Strength, Dex!!!!! You inspire me!!!!"

Marinell: "Thanks for posting the finish line video on FB so we could all experience it and be there in spirit. What a moment! What a great team! Congrats to all. Whatever I need to do or think I can't do, from now on I will say, 'If Dex can do RAAM, surely I can do this.' True inspiration!"

Ed Shepard: "Outstanding!!! Uncommon endurance and commitment. Wear your title proudly, Dex. You are a giant in the ranks of ultra cycling."

William Richard Perrin: "Congratulations Dex and Team Dex. What an amazing ride. I have been following you from Saudi Arabia all this time and my wife has been following you from Texas."

Marisol Garcia: "Wow!!!! So amazing!! Gave me chills watching the video of you crossing that finish line!!!"

Tammie Satterfield: "There are no words to describe the feeling we had here at home seeing you cross that finish line. I just have one question now. What are we supposed to do now? We have been logging onto Facebook all hours of the day and night for updates. We won't know what to do now. :D"

Brenda Beard: "GREAT, so glad they finally went live!!! LOOKING GOOD, DEX & TEAM!!!! I'm doing the Dexas Wave!!!!"

Scott Misplay: "Dex, you are an Icon here in Austin. Congrats and heal fast. To your support crew, kudos. You guys are amazing. Great job by all and thanks for taking us for a ride."

Linda Guerrette: "Dex you're a true ROCKSTAR. You've brought many people together over the course of the last 12 days. The synergy is tremendously important. As you inspire yourself you inspire others. CONGRATULATIONS!!!"

EPILOGUE

It was 5:15 in the morning and still dark as she headed to work. Yolanda Fuentes stopped at the Stripes convenience store at Veterans Boulevard and Gibbs St. to put $20.00 of unleaded in her Camry.

As she was fueling she looked over near the front door of the store and saw a bicycle leaning against a display of 12-packs of Coke. The bike had the brightest headlight she had ever seen and the taillight was flashing an eye blinding red strobe.

She recognized the bike as she had frequently seen the rider up and down Veteran's Boulevard in the early morning hours.

She heard the loud clapping noise of his cycling shoes as he came out of the store and slowly walked on the narrow sidewalk toward his bike.

She watched as he grabbed his helmet and strapped it to his head. Then he removed a small flask from his rear jersey pocket and took a hearty swig of what she imagined to be some kind of quick energy concoction.

She completed her fueling and walked toward the entrance of the store. She couldn't help but glance one more time over at him and she noticed his bright orange eyeglasses. She couldn't keep from staring.

He acknowledged her with a friendly smile as he swung his leg over his bike and clipped into the pedals.

When she got close enough for him to hear, she asked the question, "You're that guy, aren't you?"

He just smiled and said, "Yep."

AFTERWORD FROM DEX

As I come to the close of my story, I am grateful to all the readers who persevered through my undeveloped writing skills. This was my first attempt at authorship and I realize my rookie style lacked the flourish of descriptive adjectives. Heck, I even had trouble keeping my pronouns and tenses straight. But one thing I have going for me is that I have a story to tell and I cannot thank Dan Joder enough for convincing me to press forward with the book.

It took several months after the disappointment of 2010 to be able to wrap my brain around even attempting RAAM again in 2011. But I finally admitted to myself that there was no way I could accept sitting in a rocking chair 15 years down the road playing the "what if" game. I knew I would always regret it if I didn't go back and give it another shot. I finally concluded it was better to go back and possibly even fail than it was to not try at all. We are all capable of accomplishing incredible feats and I knew I had to try.

The one question that I might have neglected to give due respect to in the book is "Why?" Why do RAAM in the first place? Why does a person subject themselves to endless hours of sleep deprivation, suffering and hallucinations? Why would someone risk emergency respiratory complications, muscle failure, nerve damage and organ failure? Why does someone choose to push themselves to the edge of their physical, mental and spiritual limits?

This is probably the most-asked question I encounter and it is also the most difficult to answer. Most of the time the question is asked generically by generic fans and I give them the generic answers: "Because it is there." "Why not?" "Because I can." An answer that I have learned to use often is, "Those who ask wouldn't understand, and those who know can't explain."

But sometimes, the question of "Why?" is asked by dedicated fans who expect a very serious, if not deep, answer. To them my answer is complicated.

I can think of 100 reasons why I challenged RAAM. But I can't tell you only one. I did RAAM for the challenge, the gratification, and fulfillment. I did RAAM because I felt I had paid my dues in preparation and it was my turn. I did RAAM because of the deep desire to become a member of the very elite solo RAAM family. Maybe I even did RAAM because my inner self is some kind of sadistic nut who enjoys torture.

Months after RAAM, Joe and I were talking about this question of "Why?" After we both had exhausted our thoughts, we concluded that neither of us really knew. Furthermore, we also concluded that that was okay. Sometimes you don't have to know why you do things—you just do them. Why did I do RAAM? Because just thinking about RAAM makes the hair stand up on the back of my neck!

To be totally honest, the finish for me in 2011 was anticlimactic. A person would think that the satisfaction of riding my bike under that RAAM finish banner would be overwhelming; especially considering the psychological trauma I had suffered from my failure in 2010. Fred Boethling, the owner of RAAM, had told me at the Texas Hill Country 600 race in March of 2011 that when I crossed that finish line, it would absolutely be the most gratifying moment in my life—but that didn't happen for me. Maybe the horror of the dangerous traffic between Mt. Airy and Odenton had zapped my high expectations of the finish. Maybe it was my dilapidated condition due to exhaustion and sleep deprivation that stole the ultimate joy. Instead of gratification, my feeling at the finish line was more of relief. I was happy, but only happy it was over.

In the months leading up to RAAM, I would be riding on my morning commute to work on my trusty 20-year-old Trek 1400 complete with loaded panniers. On more than one occasion I visualized what it would be like to complete RAAM. I show my emotions easily and I confess that even on those lonely commute days, a lump would form in my throat as I was overwhelmed with emotion just thinking about crossing under that elusive finish banner. I would even think to myself how embarrassing it was going to be for me to be in front of all those fans crying like a baby. But I didn't have to be concerned about that at the actual finish line; there was little emotion.

Unfinished Business

That being said, please don't think that I walked away from RAAM with nothing more than nerve-damaged hands. In the months since the race, I have developed a tremendous amount of pride in my accomplishment that seems to grow on a daily basis. Joni and I continuously relive race moments and just shake our heads in amazement that we actually pulled this off.

My screensaver file on my home computer has hundreds of race photos. Sometimes I just sit and look at the finish line photos and I think to myself, *Oh my gosh! What if I hadn't made it through that last 30-hour push? What if there were no finish line photos?* I get a sickening feeling in my stomach just thinking those thoughts.

Having that feeling of total gratification at the finish line would have been only for that moment. This feeling of pride that I now possess will last forever. My hands may be injured, but my heart gladly accepts the tradeoff.

I caught my dream. I hope my adventure might in someway inspire some of you to also catch yours.

AFTERWORD FROM JONI

Now that all is said and done, I guess there are some folks who might be interested in how I, as Dex's wife *and* crew chief, survived this incredible RAAM adventure. It has been such a long journey that it is really very difficult to put it all into words. I have read every word of this book more than once as Dex and I relived RAAM over and over again through our efforts to put his story together. I believe *Unfinished Business* is quite a tale, but then I am perhaps somewhat partial as I am the one who has been married to Dex for almost 40 years. Being a part of his life has always been quite a trip—he simply loves to live life on the edge!

It is amazing how, even months later, we can just be sitting around our table discussing episodes of our RAAM experience and I will be overcome with emotion. The enormity of it all just hits me and the tears stream out. Even though I know it has all come true, it is sometimes difficult for me to even imagine what we accomplished. I am so happy and so proud we did this.

Preparing for RAAM 2011 was like being possessed, but not obsessed. I played the mistakes from RAAM 2010 over and over in my mind to figure out what we had to do to get Dex across that finish line the following year. It was like having this ugly little monkey on our backs, and we had to do whatever it took to get it off; I could not rest until I had it all planned out. I outlined a plan of action to assemble a crew and had them all well-trained before RAAM 2011. I took the role of crew chief and Dex agreed to let me take care of the details as I saw fit. I was determined to have the right equipment, supplies and, more importantly, a larger crew than we had on our first attempt. I went on every training ride and every pre-RAAM cycling event to personally ensure that Dex would be well prepared. I trained every crew member individually and hoped that I was doing things right. We were blessed that everything did in fact come together and we actually did pull it off—we finished RAAM!

Before RAAM 2011, my sister-in-law, Shirlee asked me how I could handle being crew chief. I was initially puzzled by her question, so she explained. She did not understand how I would be able to push Dex past the point of exhaustion. She did not understand how I could stand to see him suffer so and yet still make the tough decisions necessary to keep him on the bike. I guess I am not your typical wife, because I told her I would do whatever was necessary to help Dex accomplish his goal. The bottom line: I knew it was that important to him, which made it that important to me.

RAAM was certainly not easy, but it was worth it. I was involved every inch of the way and I would not trade that experience for anything in the world. I love watching Dex do what he does well and he can really ride that bicycle. He may not be the fastest, but he can stay in that saddle and go forever. I love to watch him ride, but I especially love to watch him climb the mountains. I call him a mountain goat because he makes it look easy when the grade steepens. He finds his rhythm and he just guts it out. I've watched him dig deep when it looks like he cannot ride another mile and then, like magic come to life, he will stand on the pedals and push it just a little more.

I was there, too, through the most terrifying parts of RAAM when I truly felt his life threatened. I watched him get hit by an angry driver and was there to encourage him and get him back on his bicycle. Even now I get tears in my eyes when I think about how he accomplished his dream. We were so blessed to have such a great crew willing to help us with this dream—but *he* was the one peddling that bicycle mile after mile. I am still so, so proud of what he did. Just think. He is one of only six men over the age of 60 to have ridden his bicycle almost 3000 miles across the continental United States of America in just a little over twelve days! I think that is pretty special.

As for the future, who knows what new adventure he will dream up for us next? All I know is that I plan to be there.

APPENDICES

Appendix 1

RACE ACROSS AMERICA 2011 OFFICIAL RESULTS (SOLO RACERS)

Rank	Racer (Solo Male, under 50)	Country	Time	Avg Speed
1	Christoph Strasser	Austria	8 d 8 h 6 m	14.94
2	Mark Pattison	USA	9 d 0 h 41 m	13.80
3	Marko Baloh	Slovenia	9 d 2 h 59 m	13.65
4	Alberto Blanco	USA	9 d 7 h 27 m	13.38
5	Nico Valsesia	Italy	9 d 16 h 9 m	12.88
6	Christopher Gottwald	USA	9 d 18 h 50 m	12.73
7	Paolo Aste	Italy	9 d 21 h 19 m	12.60
8	Joshua Kench	New Zealand	10 d 5 h 27m	12.18
9	Steven Perezluha	USA	10 d 8 h 0 m	12.05
10	Rainer Kiworra	Liechenstein	10d 10h 38 m	11.93
11	Thomas Lavallee	USA	10 d 15 h 30 m	11.70
12	Claudio Clarindo	Brazil	10 d 15 h 49 m	11.69
13	Donncha Cuttriss	Ireland	10 d 23 h 57 m	11.33
14	Andreas Dengler	Austria	11 d 0 h 18 m	11.31
15	Jens Glad Balchen	Norway	11 d 3 h 41 m	11.17
16	Nicholas Rice-McDonald	USA	11 d 4 h 10 m	11.15
17	Karl Haller	Switzerland	11 d 13 h 27 m	10.77
18	Geoff Brunner	USA	12 d 0 h 0 m	10.38
	Samim Rizvi	India	DNF	
	Mickey Campbell	Australia	DNF	
	Gerhard Gulewicz	Austria	DNF	
	Brett Walker	USA	DNF	

Rank	Racer (Solo Male, 50-59)	Country	Time	Avg Speed
1	Alessandro Colo	Italy	9 d 11 h 2 m	13.17
2	Nik Zeindler	Switzerland	10 d 3 h 39 m	12.27
3	Valerio Zamboni	Italy	10 d 18 h 59 m	11.54
4	Randy Mouri	USA	11 d 1 h 13 m	11.27
5	Ron Skelton	New Zealand	11 d 13 h 3 m	10.77
6	Kirk Gentle	USA	11 d 20 h 3 m	10.52
7	Rainer Popp	Germany	11 d 33 h 58	10.42
	Brian Welsch	United Kingdom	DNF	
	Marshall Reeves	USA	DNF	
	Michael McClintock	USA	DNF	
	Bachmann Hermann	Switzerland	DNF	

Rank	Racer (Solo Female, under 50)	Country	Time	Avg Speed
1	Leah Goldstein	Israel	11 d 4 h 41 m	11.13
	Caroline van den Bulk	Canada	DNF	

Rank	Racer (Solo Female, 50-59)	Country	Time	Avg Speed
1	Kathy Roche-Wallace	USA	12 d 15 h 59 m	9.83
	Debbie Tirrito	USA	DNF	
	Janet Christiansen	USA	DNF	

Rank	Racer (Solo Male, 60-69)	Country	Time	Avg Speed
1	David Jones	USA	12 d 7 h 10 m	10.13
2	Dave Elsberry	USA	12 d 16 h 7 m	9.83
3	Dex Tooke	USA	12 d 19 h 46 m	9.71

Appendix 2

RACE ACROSS AMERICA 2011 TIME STATIONS

TS #	Time Station	TS miles	Total Mileage
1	Lake Henshaw, CA	53.5	53.5
2	Brawley, CA	88.5	141.9
3	Blyth, CA	89.6	231.6
4	Parker, AZ	51.3	282.9
5	Salome, AZ	56	338.9
6	Congress, AZ	52.6	391.5
7	Prescott, AZ	50.2	441.7
8	Cottonwood, AZ	41.2	482.9
9	Flagstaff, AZ	53.2	536.1
10	Tuba city, AZ	71.8	607.9
11	Kayenta, AZ	71.8	679.7
12	Mexican Hat, UT	44.6	724.3
13	Montezuma Creek, UT	39.6	763.9
14	Cortez, CO	50.1	814
15	Durango, CO	43.7	857.7
16	Pagosa Springs, CO	54.3	912.2
17	South Fork, CO	47.8	960.1
18	Alamosa, CO	46.6	1006.7
19	La Veta, CO	58.2	1064.9

20	Trinidad, CO	65.1	1130
21	Kim, CO	71.2	1201.2
22	Walsh, CO	68.4	1269.6
23	Ulysses, KS	53.8	1323.4
24	Montezuma, KS	50.4	1373.8
25	Greensburg, KS	66.1	1439.9
26	Pratt, KS	32	1471.9
27	Maize, KS	76.8	1548.6
28	El Dorado, KS	34.2	1582.8
29	Yates Center, KS	64.5	1647.3
30	Ft. Scott, KS	59	1706.4
31	Weaubleau, MO	66.3	1772.7
32	Camdenton, MO	49	1821.7
33	Jefferson City, MO	57.1	1878.8
34	Washington, MO	76.8	1955.7
35	Mississippi River	72.6	2028.3
36	Greenville, IL	46	2074.3
37	Effingham, IL	49.3	2123.5
38	Sullivan, IN	72.7	2196.2
39	Bloomington, IN	67.3	2263.5
40	Greensburg, IN	63.2	2326.7
41	Oxford, OH	49.6	2376.3
42	Blanchester, OH	50.2	2426.5
43	Chillicothe, OH	58.1	2484.6
44	Athens, OH	59.1	2543.7
45	Ellenboro, WV	66.6	2610.3
46	Grafton, WV	64.8	2675.1
47	Keyser, WV	69.4	2744.4
48	Cumberland, MD	28.5	2772.9
49	Hancock, MD	37	2809.9
50	Rouzerville, PA	48.5	2858.3

51	Hanover, PA	40.3	2898.6
52	Mt. Airy, MD	36.6	2935.2
53	Odenton, MD	39.4	2974.6
54	Annapolis, MD	11.7	2986.3
55	Finish—Dock	3.5	2989.8

Appendix 3

TEAM DEX CREWS, RACE ACROSS AMERICA

Team Dex 2010 Crew:

I will forever be grateful for the courageous and dogged effort of the 2010 Team Dex crew. These were the trail blazers that led the way for our success in 2011:

Joni Tooke
Joe Tooke
Lisa Good
Merry Staffen
Eldon Brown
Mark Biggs
Raul Castillo
Michael Tarbet
Enrique Noriega

Team Dex 2011 Crew:

Joni Tooke:	Crew Chief, Domestique
Joe Tooke:	Navigator, Historian
Conice Boenicke:	Navigator, Medic
Dan Joder:	Navigator, Historian
Emily Cooper:	Driver
Damaris Ortega-Ford:	Driver
Michael West:	Driver, Maintenance
Anika Blanco:	Domestique
Elaine Lemp:	Domestique
Michael Tarbet:	Webmaster

APPENDIX 4

TEAM DEX PREPARATION, EQUIPMENT, NUTRITION, MEDICATION

Dex's annual training miles leading up to RAAM 2011:

Year	Total Annual Mileage	Rides over 100 miles
2006	12316	3
2007	13291	6
2008	17136	26
2009	20340	52
2010	18653	66
Jan. 2011 thru May 2011	6977	24

Dex's Ride:

- Specialized Roubaix frame
- Campy Chorus 11 components
- Topolino tubular wheel set
- Reynolds tubular wheel set
- Easton EC90 clincher wheel set
- Dinotte lighting
- Syntace Aero Bars

Nutrition:

- Ensure
- Emergen C
- Hammergel
- Bananas
- Perpetuem
- Iso-Pure
- Balance Bars
- Cliff Bars
- Daily pastas, burritos, egg sandwiches and yum yum ice cream.

Hydration:

- Endurolytes
- Pedialite
- V-8

Medication:

- Ibuprofen as needed

Joni's Special Saddle Sore Treatment Procedure:

1) Wash area with wound wash and water.
2) Apply Triple Action Antibacterial ointment to open wounds.
3) Spray Lanocaine over entire area and allow drying.
4) Spray Dermaplast over entire area and allow drying.
5) Apply generously Lanticeptic ointment to entire area.
6) Use a short liner and double cycling shorts for extra padding.

APPENDIX 5

TEAM DEX 2011 RAAM EXPENSES

Everybody always wants to know how much it all cost!

RAAM Entry Fee	$2995.00
Cycling Apparel: Shorts, Jerseys, Rain Gear, Gloves, Socks, Cold weather gear	$976.00
Bike expenses: Brooks saddle, Campy Chorus 11 components, Headlight batteries/chargers, Hydration system, Tires, Tubes, Tube tape, Helmet, Other misc. equipment	$2852.00
Miscellaneous Vehicle Set Up: Battery charger, Microphone mixer, Tire inflators, Spare wheel for Shadow, Mattresses for Bessie, Radio communications, Inverters, Fuel additives, Bessie tune up	$1294.00
Miscellaneous: Medical supplies, First aid, Portable toilets (2), Crew supplies, Groceries for Bessie, Dex's nutritional supplies	$2555.00

Unfinished Business

Team Dex Training Rides	$1204.00
Team Dex Air Fares	$850.00
Fuel Expenses for Bessie and Shadow	$4265.00
Team Dex Motels	$1971.00
Miscellaneous RAAM on the road expenses	$925.00
Post-RAAM Gratifications	$600.00
Total RAAM Expenses 2011	$20,487.00

Appendix 6

TEAM DEX 2011 RAAM COMMUNICATIONS

Communication for 2011 was a huge improvement over 2010 and I feel it was a major contributor to Team Dex success. Here were the key ingredients:

- Bluetooth Multi Interphone Headsets Intercom System (2 sets)
- Radio Shack microphone mixer with a handheld microphone.
- Set of marine speakers with amplifier
- Set of flags to signal Dex from a distance

Appendix 7

TEAM DEX 2011 RAAM VEHICLE SETUPS

Follow Vehicle (Shadow):

- Plastic drawer storage system for nutrition, clothing and equipment
- Metal bed frame with three-inch foam mattress
- Two ice chests for extra ice and storage of immediate nutrition for Dex
- Storage space for two 2 ½ gallon jugs of water
- 200-watt rice cooker with utensils
- 400-watt power inverter wired directly to the van battery
- Sound and music system: mike mixer, speakers, microphone, amplifier, MP3 player, Bluetooth headset
- Bicycle and wheel roof-mounted racks
- Backup bicycle and wheels
- Magnetic amber safety lights
- Slow moving vehicle safety triangle
- Portable camp toilet with plastic bags and toilet paper
- Two portable urinals for male and female
- Extra flashlights
- GPS system
- Set of signal flags

RV (Bessie):

- Stock of nutrition, drinks and food for Dex and crew
- Large ice chest that doubled as extra seating
- Portable backup generator
- Portable air conditioning unit
- Portable toilet for backup
- Bedding for crew
- Tools and bicycle tools
- GPS system
- Set of signal flags

Appendix 8
DEX'S SLEEP BREAKS, RAAM 2011

Sleep No.	Date	Time of day	Sleep Minutes	Location
1	15-Jun	7:35	43	Outside Brawley
2	15-Jun	18:54	60	After Parker-115 degrees
3	16-Jun	13:24	30	Cottonwood TS8
4	17-Jun	3:12	84	After Tuba City
5	18-Jun	3:36	120	Durango TS15
6	19-Jun	1:35	60	La Veta TS19
7	19-Jun	7:19	30	After Trinidad
8	20-Jun	4:47	30	After Ulysses
9	20-Jun	13:15	30	Greensburg TS25
10	21-Jun	1:00	90	El Dorado TS28
11	21-Jun	4:55	36	Outside El Dorado
13	21-Jun	16:12	60	Nevada, MO
14	22-Jun	1:45	120	Camdenton TS32
15	22-Jun	19:55	15	Detour sleep
16	23-Jun	0:00	135	Before Greenville, IL TS36
17	23-Jun	22:59	135	Past Bloomington, IN TS39
18	24-Jun	4:44	30	Before Greensburg, IN TS40
19	24-Jun	23:41	180	Chillicothe, OH TS43
20	25-Jun	5:45	15	Before McArthur, OH
21	26-Jun	2:45	120	Macomber, WV
22	27-Jun	2:52	15	Manchester, MD

1438		Total Minutes Sleep
23.97		Total Hours Sleep
1.87		Hours Sleep per 24-Hour Period

Appendix 9

DEX'S CALORIE CONSUMPTION, RAAM 2011

RAAM 2011 12 Hour Calorie Stats		
June 15 Wednesday		Total Accumulated Calories
Oceanside, CA to Parker, AZ		
Total Calories 1st 12 hours	1593	
Total Calories 2nd 12 hours	1305	
Total Daily Calories	2898	**2898**
June 16 Thursday		
Parker, AZ to Cottonwood, AZ		
Total Calories 1st 12 hours	1368	
Total Calories 2nd 12 hours	2468	
Total Daily Calories	3836	**6734**
June 17 Friday		
Cottonwood, AZ to Montezuma Creek, UT		
Total Calories 1st 12 hours	1195	
Total Calories 2nd 12 hours	2458	
Total Daily Calories	3653	**10387**

Unfinished Business

June 18 Saturday **Montezuma Creek, UT to Alamosa, CO**		
Total Calories 1st 12 hours	1650	
Total Calories 2nd 12 hours	2718	
Total Daily Calories	4368	**14755**
June 19 Sunday **Alamosa, CO to Kim, CO**		
Total Calories 1st 12 hours	2056	
Total Calories 2nd 12 hours	2910	
Total Daily Calories	4966	**19721**
June 20 Monday **Kim, CO to Maize, KS**		
Total Calories 1st 12 hours	2555	
Total Calories 2nd 12 hours	2848	
Total Daily Calories	5403	**25124**
June 21 Tuesday **Maize, KS to Camdenton, MO**		
Total Calories 1st 12 hours	2503	
Total Calories 2nd 12 hours	2717	
Total Daily Calories	5220	**30344**
June 22 Wednesday **Camdenton, MO To Mississippi River**		
Total Calories 1st 12 hours	2438	
Total Calories 2nd 12 hours	2058	
Total Daily Calories	4496	**34840**

June 23 Thursday Mississippi River to Bloomington, IN		
Total Calories 1st 12 hours	2471	
Total Calories 2nd 12 hours	3357	
Total Daily Calories	5828	**40668**
June 24 Friday **Bloomington, IN to Chillicothe, OH**		
Total Calories 1st 12 hours	1731	
Total Calories 2nd 12 hours	2773	
Total Daily Calories	4504	**45172**
June 25 Saturday **Chillicothe, OH to Grafton, WV**		
Total Calories 1st 12 hours	1788	
Total Calories 2nd 12 hours	2996	
Total Daily Calories	4784	**49956**
June 26 Wednesday **Grafton, WV to Rouzerville, PA**		
Total Calories 1st 12 hours	1550	
Total Calories 2nd 12 hours	2653	
Total Daily Calories	4203	**54159**

June 27 Wednesday Rouzerville, PA to Annapolis, MD		
Total Calories 1st 12 hours	2153	**56312**
Total Calories 2nd 12 hours	853	
Total Daily Calories		
	·	
Total RAAM Calories	56312	
Calories Per 24 Hours	4036	
Calories Per Hour of RAAM	168	

APPENDIX 10

DEX'S 12 HOUR MILEAGE CHART, RAAM 2011

My crew kept a running total of the total miles covered for each 12 hour segment of the race.

RAAM 2011 12 Hour Mileage Statistics		Total Miles
June 15 Wednesday **Oceanside, CA to Parker, AZ**		
Total miles 1st 12 hours	151	
Total miles 2nd 12 hours	138	
Total daily miles	289	**289**
June 16 Thursday **Parker, AZ to Cottonwood, AZ**		
Total miles 1st 12 hours	99	
Total miles 2nd 12 hours	109	
Total daily miles	208	**497**

June 17 Friday		
Cottonwood, AZ to Montezuma Creek, UT		
Total miles 1st 12 hours	139	
Total miles 2nd 12 hours	139	
Total daily miles	278	**775**
June 18 Saturday		
Montezuma Creek, UT to Alamosa, CO		
Total miles 1st 12 hours	119	
Total miles 2nd 12 hours	113	
Total daily miles	232	**1007**
June 19 Sunday		
Alamosa, CO to Kim, CO		
Total miles 1st 12 hours	125	
Total miles 2nd 12 hours	121	
Total daily miles	246	**1253**
June 20 Monday		
Kim, CO to Maize, KS		
Total miles 1st 12 hours	149	
Total miles 2nd 12 hours	123	
Total daily miles	272	**1525**
June 21 Tuesday		
Maize, KS to Camdenton, MO		
Total miles 1st 12 hours	136	
Total miles 2nd 12 hours	136	
Total daily miles	272	**1797**

June 22 Wednesday		
Camdenton, MO To Mississippi River		
Total miles 1st 12 hours	100	
Total miles 2nd 12 hours	134	
Total daily miles	234	**2031**
June 23 Thursday		
Mississippi River to Bloomington, IN		
Total miles 1st 12 hours	100	
Total miles 2nd 12 hours	142	
Total daily miles	242	**2273**
June 24 Friday		
Bloomington, IN to Chillicothe, OH		
Total miles 1st 12 hours	94	
Total miles 2nd 12 hours	123	
Total daily miles	217	**2490**
June 25 Saturday		
Chillicothe, OH to Grafton, WV		
Total miles 1st 12 hours	79	
Total miles 2nd 12 hours	122	
Total daily miles	201	**2691**
June 26 Wednesday		
Grafton, WV to Rouzerville, PA		
Total miles 1st 12 hours	105	
Total miles 2nd 12 hours	103	
Total daily miles	208	**2899**

June 27 Wednesday		
Rouzerville, PA to Annapolis, MD		
Total miles to finish	90.9	**2989.8**
Total Official Miles	2989.8	
307.75 Hours/Average Miles Per Hour	9.71	
Average Miles Per Day	233.21	
Official RAAM Time: 12 days 19 hours 46 minutes		

APPENDIX 11

KEY TERMS, DEFINITIONS AND ABBREVIATIONS

Bessie—Nickname of the support RV used for cooking and crew.

BFF—Best fuzzy friend, in polite company.

Century—A 100-mile race or ride. Sometimes you may hear the term "metric century" and this would be a 100-kilometer (62-mile) race or ride. To a RAAM rider, a century is but a warm-up.

Direct follow—To follow directly behind the racer with a follow vehicle, meaning within 50 feet of the racer. Direct follow was mandatory at night.

DNF—Did not finish. Swear words in the RAAM game.

Domestique—In RAAM, this has a slightly different meaning than in the pro cycling world. In RAAM, this is the person in the follow vehicle responsible for the nutrition, hydration and comfort of the racer.

Double century—A 200-mile race or ride—a nice little outing for a RAAM rider, and RAAM training building blocks.

Driver—It may sound like an easy job, but it is not. The driver must drive safely, protect and monitor the racer at all times, stay awake, and back up the navigator.

EMS—Emergency Medical Services.

Go down—To go to sleep. A tired RAAM racer doesn't merely go to sleep—he or she goes *down*.

IT—Information Technology person or, perhaps more commonly, computer geek.

Leapfrog—A type of support in which the support vehicle is not directly behind the racer but instead leapfrogs the racer at regular intervals at the speed of traffic. The support vehicle stops off the road, waits for a period of time, then catches the racer and stops again. Leapfrog was mandatory during daylight hours for the first 1000 miles of RAAM 2011.

Navigator—Person responsible for keeping the racer and crew on course. Navigation errors can be costly in both time and in terms of racer morale, so attention to the details in the RAAM *Route Book* is a must.

NPS—National Park Service. At Amistad Lake near Del Rio, Texas, a witness to many miles of my training rides.

RAAM—The Race Across America. It began in 1982 as the Great American Bike Race and the original four racers were John Marino, John Howard, Michael Shermer, and Lon Haldeman.

RAW—The Race Across the West. A shorter ultra cycling event by the same organizers, it covers the first 860 miles of the RAAM route.

Shadow—Nickname of the support van used to stay with the rider.

TS—Time Station. In RAAM, these would often be at locations where food, gas and a telephone were available. Most were unmanned. The few manned time stations were like little oases along the route.

Notable time stations:

Congress, AZ (TS6)—Jim Petter and the Bullshifters Bicycle Club

Durango, CO (TS15)—Candace Chiapusio

Camdenton, MO (TS32)—Erik Johnston

Oxford, OH (TS41)—Martin Dressman, Amy and John McFaddin

Blanchester, OH (TS42)—Martin Dressman and Jim Lawyer

Mt Airy, MD (TS52)—Larry Black and Mt Airy Bike Shop

War Room—The RAAM headquarters in Tucson, Arizona, manned 24/7. The officials there are responsible for monitoring the progress and safety of all racers on the course as well as adjusting the route in cases of pop-up problems—construction, storm, accidents, flooding, etc.

Made in the USA
San Bernardino, CA
10 December 2013